PROPHETS OF DOOM

PROPHETS OF DOOM

THE MILLENNIUM EDITION

DANIEL COHEN

THE MILLBROOK PRESS
BROOKFIELD, CONNECTICUT

Published by The Millbrook Press, Inc.
2 Old New Milford Road
Brookfield, CT 06804

Photographs courtesy of © The British Museum: p. 11; Old Economy Village: p. 22; AP/ Wide World Photos: pp. 24, 146; from *Days of Delusion*: p. 28; New York Public Library Collection: pp. 40, 50, 134; Author's collection: pp. 57, 69, 72, 81, 86, 95, 99, 121, 123, 125, 139; from *Spirits, Stars and Spells*: p. 61; Photo Researchers: p. 111 (© Calvin Larsen); U.S. Geological Survey: p. 130; Lookout Mountain Laboratory, USAF: p. 136

Library of Congress Cataloging-in-Publication Data
Cohen, Daniel, 1936–
Prophets of doom / by Daniel Cohen. — Millennium ed.
p. cm.
Includes bibliographical references and index.
Summary: Examines prophecies from the Bible, Greek oracles, Nostradamus, and Edgar Cayce, particularly those dealing with the end of the world.
ISBN 0-7613-1317-6 (lib. bdg.)
1. Prophets—History. 2. End of the world—Miscellanea. 3. Prophecies (Occultism)—History. [1. Prophets. 2. End of the world. 3. Prophecies (Occultism)] I. Title.
BF1791.C59 1999
133.3—dc21 98-38462 CIP AC

CONTENTS

1
THE END IS NEAR
9

2
HOW THE WORLD ENDED IN 1844
26

3
LIFTING THE VEIL
38

4
OMENS AND PORTENTS
47

5
THE PUZZLE OF PROPHECY
54

6
NOSTRADAMUS
66

7
THE SLEEPING PROPHET AND OTHERS
79

8
PYRAMIDS AND SPACESHIPS
90

9
THE DOOMSDAY ROCK
105

10
SIGNS IN THE SKY AND THE EARTH
118

11
THE FOUR HORSEMEN
132

12
TOWARD THE YEAR 2000
142

SELECTED BIBLIOGRAPHY
154

INDEX
157

PROPHETS
OF
DOOM

In the year 1530 the German city of Munster was taken over by a religious sect known as the Anabaptists. This was an era of tremendous religious turmoil, but the Anabaptists of Munster were extreme, even in an age of extremes. They believed that the world as we know it was about to come to an end. Because they found the world around them to be hopelessly sinful and corrupt, they wanted to see it end as quickly as possible. In order to hasten the end, they were going to turn their city into the New Jerusalem—the place where Christ would return to earth.

The first order of business was to "purify" the city of Munster—they expelled all the Catholics and Lutherans and everyone else who disagreed with them. Thus the Anabaptists proved that they could be just as intolerant of others as others had been of them.

Very soon powerful forces were raised against the Anabaptists, and the city was surrounded by a large army led by the former bishop of Munster. The leader of the Munster Anabaptists, Jan Matthys, believed he had received a divine command to break the siege of the city with a handful of men. The small group set out and was immediately cut to pieces, and Matthys was killed.

The leadership of Munster was then taken over by Matthys's young disciple, Jan Bockelson. He is known to history as John of Leiden, for that is the city from which he originally came. This new leader was more fanatical than the first. He assumed the title Messiah of the Last Days.

While the people of Munster had been reduced to starvation and despair, John of Leiden and his associates went about in magnificent robes, their comings and goings heralded by the blowing of trumpets. It would be quite wrong to conclude that John was a cynical fraud who was exploiting his followers. Both the leader and his people were living out a powerful fantasy. As ridiculous and insane as it looks to us, it was absolutely real to them.

But of course, it was a fantasy. And on June 24, 1535, the fantasy was shattered. Two Anabaptist deserters led the besiegers through the defenses of Munster in a surprise attack. The hopelessly outnumbered Anabaptists fought ferociously, and the few hundred survivors surrendered only after they were promised safe conduct to their homes. The promise was immediately broken and the survivors slaughtered.

John of Leiden, the self-proclaimed Messiah of the Last Days, was publicly tortured to death. Throughout the ordeal he never uttered a word.

In the mistaken conviction that the world was about to end, John of Leiden led the Anabaptists in a bloody takeover of the German city of Munster.

What makes people behave as John of Leiden and his followers did? There are many reasons, not all of them known or understood. But clearly one very powerful reason is an unshakable conviction that the world is in its Last Days and that very soon the world as we know it will be destroyed and everything will be changed in one grand and cataclysmic stroke.

Even today some of the beliefs and feelings that inspired the Anabaptists of Munster to such heroism, and madness, are still with us. There is no reason to believe that another Messiah of the Last Days will take over a city, but there is a good deal of talk about the Last Days.

Where does such a belief come from, and why has it persisted for so long?

The belief that the world will end or be totally changed suddenly, and probably very soon, comes right out of Western religious tradition. The belief figures prominently in both the Old and the New Testament. The Jews have always awaited the coming of the Messiah who would appear to save them, punish their enemies, and change the world. The Hebrew prophets Daniel, Enoch, Moses, and Baruch all helped to sustain the faith of their people in difficult, often desperate times with pronouncements of the coming of the Messiah.

Around the time of Jesus, hopes and expectations for the coming Messiah were particularly high. Some Jews came to believe that Jesus was the Messiah. Others continued to wait.

At least in part because they believed that the Messiah would come to save them, the Jews raised the standard of revolt against the mighty Romans. The revolt was doomed from the start and utterly crushed in A.D. 70. The Romans captured Jerusalem and burned the Temple, the most sacred of all Jewish holy sites. To many, that seemed such an appalling event that it would certainly bring about the coming of the Messiah. But nothing happened. The Temple has not been rebuilt to this day.

Though the Christians had their Messiah, the sense that the world would end was, if anything, even stronger among them. Early Christians faced persecution, death, and the possible extinction of their new religion. The New Testament fairly bristles with references to the coming end of the world. When Jesus was asked what would be the signs of his return and the coming end, he replied: "Ye shall hear wars and rumors of wars. . . . The sun shall be darkened and the moon shall not give her light, and the stars shall fall from heaven, and the powers of the heavens shall be shaken" (Matthew 24:6-30).

What will the end of the world be like? Peter makes the picture depressingly vivid: "The heavens shall pass away with a great noise and the elements shall melt with fervent heat, the earth also and the worlds that are therein shall be burned up"(2 Peter 3:10).

The final book of the New Testament is an account of the revelation attributed to Saint John on the island of Patmos, to which he had been exiled by the Roman emperor Domitian, a ferociously anti-Christian emperor. The Book of Revelation, often called the Apocalypse, is one of the most forceful yet puzzling parts of the New Testament. The word *apocalypse* means revelation and more specifically a vision of how the world will end. The revelation of Saint John is only one of a whole body of apocalyptic works produced by prophetic writers of the time. All of these writings share a similar poetic language and use grand and striking images that are memorable yet difficult to penetrate.

The Bible sets no date for the end. Indeed, Jesus warned specifically of the folly of trying to determine the exact time: "Of that day or that hour no one knows, not even the angels in heaven, nor the son, but only the Father" (Mark 13:32). But from the earliest days of Christianity, right up to the present time, many Christians have believed that clues to the exact time of the end of the world can be found scattered throughout the Old and New Testament. All that is needed is for the sometimes puzzling phrases to be interpreted and put together properly. It is the search for the meaning of prophetic messages in the Bible that makes up the single most important element in today's doomsday prophecies.

Different cultures have had different ideas about the end of the world. Some, like the Hindus, see the world going through an endless cycle of deaths and rebirths—with each phase of the cycle being unimaginably long. But those of us who live in late-twentieth-century America or Europe have been most heavily influenced by the biblical view of what will happen to the world, and most specifically by the Christian view that the end of the world is coming soon.

The influence is there whether we are Christians or not. It is not simply a religious view anymore; it is a part of Western culture. No matter what our background and beliefs, we have all heard that the world is going to come to a catastrophic end soon, and we have heard that repeatedly. It has stuck somewhere in the back of our minds, whether we want it there or not. We had all better know where it came from, and why it is such a powerful belief.

To the earliest Christians, Judgment Day was not a distant event. They believed that Jesus would return soon—within their own lifetimes. And this Second Coming or Second Advent would set in motion a series of events leading to the end of the world as we know it.

Saint Paul described the return of Christ in vivid terms. Then he said, "The dead in Christ will rise first; and then *we who remain alive* shall be caught up together with them in the clouds to meet the Lord in the air" (I Thessalonians 4:16).

It appears that Paul expected some of those who heard his words, some of his own contemporaries, to still be alive on Judgment Day. The sense of urgency, that the moment was at hand, is inescapable.

Early Christian communities saw little need for long-range planning in any sense except a religious one, since they were sure that the end of the world was, at most, just a few years away. This belief filled the early Christians with a fervor to proselytize—to bring the Christian message to as many people as possible, as quickly as possible, because the time was short. It was a belief that gave individuals enormous courage and great inspiration and tremendous energy. Everything had to be done *now*; there was no time to waste!

But as time went on, the world failed to end, while the number and power of the Christians grew. Christians, who had once been a tiny persecuted minority hovering on the edge of extinction, were forced to make more and more accommodations to a world in which they were increasingly powerful and prosperous. They had to start making plans to preserve and add to what they had gained in this world.

Still, it was several centuries before the main body of Christians was able to abandon the idea that the end of the world was right around the corner. In the middle of the second century A.D., the Christian writer Justian told how he expected the Second Coming within his own lifetime, but he did admit that not all Christians agreed with this point of view anymore.

During the second century A.D., many Christians had more or less decided that the world would end six thousand years after the Creation. At that time, the conventional date for the Creation was set at 5500 B.C.; thus 5,700 years had passed. These dates were decided on by totaling up various time references in the Bible. The references are not exact, but the desire to set a date for the Creation as well as for the End is one that has captured many biblical scholars for centuries.

In 1650 the very learned Archbishop James Ussher of Ireland collected all of the age references in the Old Testament. From these he calculated that the earth had been created in the year 4004 B.C. It was later than the 5500 B.C. date of the early scholars, but it was in the same general range. Bishop Ussher's date became widely accepted. The date appeared printed in the margin of the first chapter of Genesis in many copies of the Bible for years. Some biblical scholars refined the time to an even finer point, calculating that the Creation began at nine in the morning of October 24, 4004 B.C.

For the second-century Christian who believed that the earth had existed for 5,700 of its allotted 6,000 years, it meant that the world would endure another three hundred years. Today scientists estimate that the earth is 4.5 *billion* years old. So three hundred years doesn't seem like very much. But for early Christians, who had been accustomed to the view that the world would come to an end at any moment, three centuries seemed like an enormous amount of time. It became increasingly necessary to make peace with the world, rather than living as though at any moment it was going to disappear in a burst of flame.

Not all Christians took this reprieve for the world joyfully. A number of sects clung to the belief in an imminent apocalypse. Generally, apocalyptic sects had the greatest appeal among the poor and desperate, those who had little or nothing to lose in this world. These were the people for whom life in this world held little appeal or hope. They saw nothing but injustice and immorality all around them and despaired that the world could ever be reformed. Evil people seemed to be prospering while they were starving. They had no power to change the world. It was just going to get worse and worse, and the only thing they could look forward to was the great and terrible day when Christ would return and all the accounts would be settled. For all its terror, there is something very satisfying about a vision of the apocalypse, particularly when you feel you have nothing to look forward to.

A typical apocalyptic movement, Montanism, was started in the second century by a recently baptized Christian named Montanus. Montanus would go into a trance and utter prophecies about how the heavenly city of Jerusalem was soon to descend to earth, and this would be the signal for the Second Coming. Montanus was joined by two equally inspired prophetesses, and they began to gather a large following. Because they saw the end of the world at hand, they actually sought out martyrdom. The Romans were usually more than willing to oblige them.

Historian Norman Cohn described Montanus thus:

> *The new prophet's personality and eloquence won him a host of disciples, who flocked in such numbers to the appointed spot that a new town sprang up around them. Nor did the delay of the second advent put an end to the movement. On the contrary it gave it new life and form as a kind of Christianity of the elite, whom no other authority guided in the new life but the Holy Spirit working directly up them.*

Montanism outlived its prophets and for a while threatened to create a serious split in the Christian world. Ultimately it could not outlive the stubborn fact that the world failed to end. The movement declined and disappeared. But the forces that inspired it have never disappeared.

Most Christians finally abandoned even the six-thousand-year life span for the world and stopped making any attempt to set an exact date for the world to end. They stressed the biblical passages that say no one can know the time or the hour of the Second Coming over those passages that seemed to indicate that the end was very near. It was not that these Christians abandoned the idea of an apocalyptic end for the world as we know it; they just assumed that the date would be sometime in the distant future. It could happen at any moment—but probably wouldn't. Increasing attention was paid to the maintenance and preservation of the Christian community in an unchanged world.

Yet the appeal of the apocalyptic remained enormous. In the third century it was the followers of Novatian who became the primary supporters of the apocalyptic tradition. His followers cried: "Come Lord Christ, clothed in all thy wrath and judgement, come with all thy vengeance, come!"

In the fourth century the leading apocalyptists were the followers of the prophecies of Donatus of North Africa. The Donatists reminded the faithful that those specially chosen by the Lord would number only 144,000. This number was drawn from the Book of Revelation: "I looked and lo, a Lamb stood on Mount Zion, and with him a hundred and forty thousand, having his Father's name written on their foreheads" (Revelation 14:1).

Like Montanus and Novatian, Donatus was also denounced as a heretic, and his movement was ultimately crushed. But the spirit survived. There were the Anabaptists, like those of Munster described at the beginning of this chapter. There were other groups with names like Waldensians, Albigenses, Moravian Brethren—apocalyptic advocates all. And the chain remains unbroken to the present day. Just turn on your television set: If you happen to get any one of a number of cable television channels that run religious programming, you are more than likely to find someone addressing his or her audience in much the same terms that Montanus used to preach to his followers nearly two thousand years ago.

Today apocalyptic preachers may be criticized or ridiculed, but they are tolerated. In the past they were often fiercely persecuted as heretics. Therefore it is natural that a large number of them in Europe were attracted to the relative religious freedom offered by the New World. We like to think of early immigrants to America as looking for a place where they could build a new life and a bright future. But a surprisingly large number came in hope of finding a place where they could await the end of the world in peace. America has an exceptionally rich history of apocalyptic movements.

One of the first apocalyptic groups to come to America was also one of the most curious. It was based on the ideas of an ex-Lutheran preacher, Johann Jacob Zimmerman, who mixed theology and astrology and calculated that the world would come to an end in the autumn of 1694. He was anxious to get to the New World where he could greet the return of Christ in the wilderness.

According to Zimmerman, the wilderness was the best place to greet the returning Christ. He had determined this after reading the Book of Revelation, where it was written that the true Church, symbolized by a woman, was given "two wings of a great eagle, that she might fly into the wilderness, into her place, where she is nourished for a time and times, and half a time from the face of the serpent" (Revelation 12:14).

Zimmerman and a group of disciples prepared to depart for the wilderness of America in February 1694. On the very day of departure, the prophet died. Leadership of the little group passed to twenty-one-year-old Johannes Kelpius, an immensely learned young man who, like Zimmerman, had combined Christianity with a host of mystical, pagan, and just plain superstitious beliefs and practices.

Once in America the little band of brothers headed for the wilderness of Pennsylvania and began constructing their Tabernacle. It was a wooden building that measured 40 feet square and contained forty cells for the forty brethren. Forty was clearly a number that had great mystical significance. Over the door they placed the symbol of the rose and the cross, which was believed to be the emblem of a secret occult society called the Rosicrucians. On the roof of the Tabernacle they mounted a telescope so that they might better observe the signs of the coming end that were to appear in the heavens. Kelpius, being even more of a hermit than his followers, did not live in the Tabernacle, but in a nearby cave. The little community became known as The Woman in the Wilderness—that is, The Church in the Wilderness.

The autumn of 1694 came and went and the world survived. The brethren were deeply disappointed. Time after time they believed they had witnessed unmistakable signs of the coming end. In each instance they had to admit that they were wrong. Members began to drift away. Kelpius himself died in 1708, after having abandoned all hope that the Second Advent would take place within his lifetime. The community itself continued to exist in one form or another for several decades.

It would be a great mistake to write off these apocalyptists as a group of deluded fools who just sat around gazing through their telescope and waiting for the world to end. Like many other apocalyptic groups before and since, they were extraordinarily active in a variety of ways. Aside from generally raising the educational level of the community of German immigrants who were their nearest neighbors, they also printed the first book of music in America and compiled an invaluable vocabulary of Indian words. This last effort was the result of their attempt to evangelize the Indians. The brethren, like many other Bible students of their day, were convinced that the American Indians were the direct descendants of the Ten Lost Tribes of Israel.

Lest you think that all the apocalyptists were as grim and mystical as the brethren of The Woman in the Wilderness, consider the case of the Harmony Society, better known as the Rappites. These followers of "Father" George Rapp came to America from Germany in 1804.

Although they were absolutely convinced that the world would end soon, they established a string of successful and prosperous communities. They didn't spend a lot of time preparing for the end of the world or worrying about it. They worked hard, but not too hard, for they believed that work should be a pleasure and not a punishment. They ate well and even drank alcohol in moderation. The Rappites operated the Golden Rule Distillery, which was famed for

George Rapp at the age of eighty.

its excellent whiskey. All visitors to Rappite communities were struck by the cheerfulness and good health of the members.

One thing the Rappites had to give up was sex. If the world was going to end soon, there seemed no need for children. The Rappites, however, had no rigid provisions to enforce this rule. They said that such action would be of no use: "If you have to watch people, you had better give up on them." The Rappites also had to abandon tobacco.

One observer commented that this seemed to be almost as hard for them as giving up sex.

"Father" Rapp, the likable, practical, and sensible leader of the group, was still utterly convinced that Christ would reappear before he died. Father Rapp lived on and on in great good health and cheerfulness until the age of ninety. When he finally took sick he said, "If I did not know that the dear Lord meant I should present you all to Him, I should think my last moment's come." Those were his final words.

One apocalyptic group of recent times was led by David Koresh. He was the leader of the Branch Davidians—a tiny radical offshoot of the Seventh-Day Adventists. He believed that the End Times were upon us, and that the final struggle between the forces of good and evil was about to begin, a struggle in which he and his followers were to play a key role.

The Branch Davidians were living in a compound near Waco, Texas, that Koresh called, all too appropriately, "Ranch Apocalypse." They were stockpiling weapons apparently in anticipation of an assault by the enemies of God. This is what brought them to the attention of the U.S. government.

On February 28, 1993, agents of the Bureau of Alcohol, Tobacco and Firearms (ATF), the federal agency that regulates weapons' sales, raided the compound in an attempt to arrest Koresh, but the Davidians had been tipped off about the raid and were armed and ready. There was a shootout in which four ATF agents and an unknown number of Davidians were killed.

That event marked the beginning of a siege that lasted fifty-one days. During the siege, Koresh issued a series of

This is a 1981 Associated Press file photo of David Koresh, taken in the Mount Carmel compound that was later burned to the ground.

manifestos filled with apocalyptic language and images; it seemed as if he was waiting for a particular day. At one point a small number of those who had been inside the compound left—but the siege continued, and topped the nightly news regularly for weeks. Finally, on April 19, U.S. authorities decided they had waited long enough. The officials sent an armored tank loaded with nonlethal tear gas rumbling toward the compound. The hope was that this show of force would get the Davidians to surrender. Failing that, tear gas would be pumped into the compound buildings, forcing the cultists into the open where they could be captured.

What happened was far worse than anyone could have imagined. Within a few moments the wooden buildings caught fire. David Koresh and some eighty of his followers, many of them with young children, died in the inferno.

What is now called the Waco tragedy has been the subject of tremendous controversy. The government insists the Davidians themselves started the fire, resolving to die in a mass suicide. Mass suicides are not unknown in apocalyptic groups. Others say the tragedy was the result of government carelessness. The gas was highly flammable, the buildings were made of wood, and there was a dry wind blowing. A spark could have touched off the gas. A few think the government, for its own sinister reasons, deliberately burned down the compound and killed those inside.

Waco has become a symbol for some apocalyptically minded groups in America. The echoes of the tragedy continue to reverberate throughout the land.

HOW THE WORLD ENDED IN 1844

2

As we have seen, there have been plenty of prophets who predicted that the end of the world would come "soon." Few, however, were bold enough to set an exact date. One who did was a New York State farmer named William Miller, and what happened to him, and to those who followed his lead, holds a lesson for us all.

Miller was no wild-eyed fanatic, no sinister cult leader. He was a simple, Bible-believing farmer from a small town near the Vermont border. In the year 1816 he decided on a course of intensive Bible study, so that he wouldn't be embarrassed by any lack of knowledge.

After two years he felt that he not only knew the Bible, but that he had also discovered something of great significance that had gone unnoticed by others.

He wrote: "I was thus brought in 1818, at the close of my two years' study of the Scriptures, to the solemn conclusion, that in about twenty-five years from that time all the affairs of our present state would be wound up."

The specific passage that gave him his inspiration occurs in the Book of Daniel: "And he said unto me, Unto two thousand and three hundred days; then shall the sanctuary be cleansed" (8:14).

The "cleansing" of the "sanctuary" could only mean the purging of the earth by fire—in short, the end of the world, Judgment Day, the Second Advent, the Second Coming of Christ was at hand. It was a glorious vision. The trumpets would blow, the sky would roll back to reveal the heavenly host, and the graves would give up their dead; all the righteous would go to heaven, and the sinners would be cast down to hell.

But when was this to happen? As many interpreters of the Bible had done before him, Miller decided that "days" really meant "years." The prophecy itself was dated at about 457 B.C.; thus the end of the two thousand and three hundred "days" would come about 1843. There had been numerous changes in the calendar over two thousand years, so Miller was unable to decide on the exact day or even the exact year in which the prophecy was to be fulfilled. But he was convinced that the "sanctuary" would be "cleansed" around the year 1843.

There was nothing at all unusual about Miller's belief that the world would come to an end "soon." It was a belief shared by many of his devout neighbors. Indeed, the upstate New York area in which Miller lived was noted for its religious fervor. It had been swept by the fires of so many religious movements and revivals that it came to be called

William Miller, who saw doomsday in the Book of Daniel.

the "Burnt Over District." The difference was that Miller was one of the very few who presumed to know the date of the great and awful event.

In addition to his interpretation of Scripture, Miller found signs of the approaching end everywhere. He wrote: "Finding all the signs of the times and the present condition of the world, to compare harmoniously with the prophetic descriptions of the last days, I was compelled to believe that this world had about reached the limits of the period allotted for its continuance. As I regarded the evidence, I could arrive at no other conclusion."

Miller did not immediately rush out to proclaim his discovery. He spent years checking and rechecking his proofs. He studied other prophetic references in the Bible. He made elaborate charts comparing the Hebrew and modern calendars. Everything pointed to the same conclusion. The world would end around 1843.

He began to discuss his ideas with a few close friends. It wasn't until 1831 that he began to speak out publicly on the subject. He had a horror of public speaking, but he felt compelled to make his "truths" known. His first speech at a small church was well received, and more invitations for speeches followed.

During the next eight years, Miller became something of a local celebrity with his lectures about biblical prophecy and the end of the world. He made converts, and the term "Millerite" became common in parts of New England and upstate New York. In 1839, Miller gave his first talk in Boston, and he converted an influential Boston clergyman to his cause. This changed Millerism from a small rural phenomenon to a mass movement of hundreds of thousands with large organized groups in most of the cities of the Northeast. There were huge outdoor camp meetings where thousands gathered to hear "Prophet" Miller preach and to engage in almost nonstop prayer sessions.

Miller and his most devout followers needed only their Bibles to convince them that the end was near. Others looked for signs of the end in the world around them, and they found plenty.

In November 1833, when Millerism was first getting started, there was a remarkably bright meteorite shower. One rural newspaper correspondent wrote: "We pronounce the raining of fire which we saw on Wednesday morning last, an awful type, a sure forerunner—a merciful sign of the great and dreadful day which the inhabitants of the earth will witness when the Sixth Seal shall be opened. The time is just at hand described, not only in the New Testament, but in the Old. A more correct picture of a fig tree casting its leaves when blown by a mighty wind is not possible to behold." The reference was to the Book of Revelation in the Bible: "And the stars of heaven fell unto earth, even as a fig tree casteth her untimely figs, when she is shaken of a mighty wind" (6:13). This was one of the signs of the approaching end of the world.

As the fateful year of 1843 opened, there occurred an even more striking and seemingly unmistakable sign in the heavens. It was the sudden and unexpected appearance of an extremely bright comet. And there were all the usual rumors of wars, famines, earthquakes, plagues, and rampant immorality that are supposed to be signals of the End Times.

While Miller had his followers, he also had his opponents, lots of them. Miller was denounced as a madman or a charlatan or both. His followers were supposed to be weak-minded folk, many of whom were actually committed to insane asylums after attending Millerite meetings. There were also charges that Millerite leaders cheated their followers out of huge sums of money.

Whatever one thinks of Miller and his beliefs, such extreme charges are unsupportable. Far from becoming rich, most Millerite leaders invested everything they possessed in the movement. The majority of those who followed the movement were farmers, small businessmen, and laborers, generally from conservative Protestant backgrounds. Millerites were the sort of hardworking, God-fearing people who were considered the backbone of nineteenth-century America. There may have been madmen among them, but no more than in the general population.

Why did they flock to Millerism in such great numbers? First, they held the belief common to all Christians that there will be a Judgment Day. Although the Bible explicitly states that no definite time can be set for Judgment Day, as we have seen there is an urgency in many biblical passages that makes it sound as if the day will be sooner rather than later. Then there was, and still is, the belief that certain passages in the Bible provide prophetic insights into the future if only the passages can be interpreted properly.

And there was more. There existed among the Millerites a strong feeling that the world *should* end. They looked around and saw only sin and wickedness and despaired that the world could ever be reformed. There was a profound weariness with the day-to-day cares and frustrations of life. If the slate were wiped clean, the sinners would be punished and the righteous rewarded. Like all who eagerly await Judgment Day, the Millerites were quite sure they were the righteous and they would go to heaven. Those foolish enough to ignore their message—or worse yet, make fun of it—would burn. In the words of a Millerite hymn:

We, while the stars from heaven shall fall,
And mountains are on mountains hurled,
Shall stand unmoved amidst them all,
And smile to see a burning world.

The earth and all the works therein
Dissolve, but raging flames destroyed;
While we survey the awful scene,
And mount above the fiery void.

31

This picture of the Millerites actually enjoying the destruction of the world, and the torment of everyone else, reveals an unsympathetic side to the movement, one that it shared with many other apocalyptic groups.

While Miller had calculated that the world would end about the year 1843, he wasn't able to set an exact date; as the fateful year approached, this began to cause some problems for the Millerites. On January 1, 1843, Miller wrote: "I am fully convinced that sometime between March 21st, 1843, and March 21st, 1844, according to the Jewish mode of computation of time, Christ will come, and bring all His Saints with Him; and He will reward every man as his work shall be."

There was a rumor that the date would be April 23, but the day passed uneventfully. Millerite leaders quite properly pointed out that they had never endorsed that particular date and that it had been given publicity mainly by their enemies.

When the calendar year of 1843 ended uneventfully, there was a more serious moment of disappointment for the followers of William Miller. But they recalled the prophet's earlier statement that the critical period could be extended as far as March 21, 1844. In fact, the months between January and March of 1844 actually saw an increase in activity and a flood of new converts to the Millerite ranks.

But when March 21, 1844, came and went without any signs that the world was about to experience the Second Coming, the Millerites faced a real crisis of faith—and a torrent of ridicule.

Miller was as puzzled and disappointed as any of his followers. He did not make any excuses for his mistaken date, but he did not give up his faith that the end was near: "I confess my error, and acknowledge my disappointment; yet I still believe that the day of the Lord is near, even at the door . . . I will try to be patient . . . I want you, my Brethren, not to be drawn away from the truth."

During the spring the movement was at a low ebb, but by the summer it had regained momentum. Miller was preaching to larger audiences than ever and planning to send missionaries to Europe.

The final date still remained a problem. A man named Samuel S. Snow had calculated that the critical date would be October 22, 1844. This date rapidly became the focus of all the Millerite hopes and dreams. Most of the major Millerite leaders were at first taken aback by the development of a movement within a movement. But one by one they declared for the October 22 date. Miller himself returned to his Bible to recalculate his original prediction. On October 6, just a little more than two weeks before the world was supposed to end, William Miller announced that he too had accepted Snow's calculations: "Now, blessed be the name of the Lord, I see a beauty, a harmony, and an agreement in the Scriptures, for which I have long prayed, but did not see until today. Thank the Lord. . . . I am almost home. Glory! Glory!! Glory!!!"

From top to bottom the Millerite movement was now fully committed to October 22, 1844. There could be no refiguring of the date this time.

Some Millerites sold all their worldly goods to give their money to the movement or to pay outstanding debts that they did not wish to leave unpaid on Judgment Day. Most did not take such a radical step.

There are stories that on the Great Day the Millerites

put on white robes, called ascension robes, and trooped to the hillsides or other high places to await the arrival of the Lord with much crying and shouting. There were even accounts of Millerites who tried to fly bodily to heaven, by jumping in the air.

There may have been a few authentic cases of such activity, but very few. The vast majority of the followers of William Miller spent October 22, 1844—the day they fervently believed to be the last of earth's existence—calmly in their homes or in the temples they had built. They wore no special robes; they did not shriek and jump in the air and try to fly. Mostly they prayed or meditated quietly and sang hymns.

The expectations of the Millerites were high as they waited for their "coming Lord until the clock tolled twelve at midnight." Instead of being relieved when the deadline passed and the world was not destroyed, the Millerites faced a disillusionment and disappointment of crushing magnitude. Wrote one: "The effect of this disappointment can be realized only by those who experienced it."

Now they had to again return to an imperfect, trouble-filled world:

> *And now to turn again to the cares, perplexities, and dangers of life, in full view of jeering and reviling unbelievers who scoffed as never before, was a terrible trial of faith and patience. Everyone felt lonely, with hardly a desire to speak to anyone. Still the cold world! No deliverance.*

Millerism had already withstood several changes of the predicted date of when the world would end, and the movement had come back stronger. But this was too much. Miller once again confessed his error about the date and expressed his great surprise and disappointment. But he held fast to the faith that the Second Coming could not be delayed by more than a few months. There were a number of ways in which he could have refigured the date, but he did not do so. Miller himself died a sad and broken man in 1849. By that time the movement that had borne his name was virtually extinct.

Some former Millerites felt betrayed and turned on their old faith with a particular fury. Many others clung to the powerful belief that the end was near. Millerism as a name disappeared, but its heritage was the movement known as Adventism. A group of one-time Millerites met in 1845 and decided that the Second Coming had indeed taken place as predicted, but only in heaven, and was thus invisible to earthly eyes. However, the return of Christ to earth might take place at any moment, though they were no longer so rash as to set an exact date. The Adventist movement is now rather fragmented. The largest group is the Seventh-Day Adventists, which has several hundred thousand deeply committed members. David Koresh's Branch Davidians were a tiny and radical offshoot of the Seventh-Day Adventists. Koresh himself had been captivated by Adventist-sponsored "Revelation Seminars," which featured dramatic, even frightening images in a multimedia portrayal of Armageddon.

An even larger, though less direct, offspring of the Millerite movement is the group known as Jehovah's Witnesses. The organization has well over a million members and may be one of the fastest-growing religious groups in the country. They are aggressive proselytizers and from time to time have been severely persecuted in countries where there is little or no religious tolerance. It is hard to imagine that there is any home in America that has not been visited by members of the group, preaching the gospel and passing out literature.

The Witnesses themselves say that they have no earthly founder. Outside observers of the movement say it really began with a Pennsylvania clothing-store owner named Charles Taze Russell (1825–1916). Russell had been profoundly influenced by Adventism. Though Russell never stated flatly when he thought the world was going to end, some of his followers interpreted his statements to mean that the end of the world would come in 1914. Russell never endorsed this date, but he never disputed it either. For a while it looked as if he was going to be right, for that is when World War I broke out. The world survived that terrible war as it has survived terrible wars in the past.

Russell himself lived only until 1916, and after his death his followers concluded that he had been right all along—the end of the world had begun in heaven in 1914. Christ had driven the devils out of the invisible world, and they had come to dwell upon earth, to punish man for his sins. That, they said, was why the moral and political climate of the earth seemed to be deteriorating.

Russell's successor, the man who invented the name Jehovah's Witnesses and who really built the movement into what it is today, was Judge J. F. Rutherford of Missouri. The Witnesses also hesitate setting dates for the end of the world, though there are rumors that a number of dates, including 1972, have been discussed within the movement. No exact date has ever been officially adopted or acknowledged by the Witnesses. Today the Witnesses seem to put less stress on the apocalypse than they did in the past. At one time they believed that on Judgment Day many of the biblical patriarchs would walk the streets of America. The Witnesses even built a grand mansion for them in San Diego. It was called Beth-Sarim, "The House of Princes," and was supposed to be inhabited by the likes of Moses and Daniel. In fact, it was inhabited by Judge Rutherford until his death in 1942, when it was finally sold.

Judge Rutherford popularized the statement "Millions Now Living Will Never Die." It became the motto of the Witnesses, though it is not nearly as prominent in their literature and advertising as it once was. Such a statement can be interpreted in many ways. The most obvious interpretation is that it represents a belief that the end of the world and Judgment Day will come within the span of this generation. The statement, however, was first popularized well over a generation ago, and the time is drawing short when any literal interpretation of these words will be possible.

Like other apocalyptic movements that have been around for a long time, the Witnesses seem more and more willing to set the apocalypse at some indefinite future date. They have even discussed what will happen to people from earth who might be on the moon or other planets when the end comes. Their conclusion was that the people will be judged wherever they are. While still searching for signs of the end, Jehovah's Witnesses also seem ready to dig in for a relatively long stay on an unfriendly but undestroyed earth.

LIFTING
THE
VEIL

3

William Miller and his followers tried to predict the future of the world by interpreting passages in the Bible. But throughout human history practically every society has tried, in one way or another, to lift the veil that appears to hide the knowledge of what is to come.

In order to help us understand why, as the twentieth century draws to a close, so many people feel that there may be no twenty-first century, it's very helpful to look backward and find out how and why other people at other times tried to see the future. In one way or another, many ancient beliefs and practices still influence us today.

The Greeks, just about everyone will agree, were the most clever people of the ancient world. They brought us democracy, drama, science, and lots of other things. They did not invent prophecy, but they were certainly interested in it. One might say they were often obsessed by it. And the Greeks produced the most influential prophets of their time.

For centuries one of the world's great power centers was a shrine on the flanks of Mount Parnassus in Greece, just north of Athens. It was a temple complex dedicated to the god Apollo, but it is better known to history as the Oracle at Delphi. The word *oracle* can mean a prophetic statement, the individual who delivers the prophecy, or the place where the prophecy is delivered. In the case of Delphi it meant all three.

Delphi was a sacred site long before the Greeks worshiped Apollo. Later the story was told that Delphi was the place where the gods killed a monster called the Python. A temple was built atop the spot where the monster was buried, and vapors from the rotting carcass inspired prophetic utterances from the priestess of Apollo. The priestess of the shrine was called the Pythia, from the word *Python.*

It is a curious fact that women have played a large role in the history of prophecy. In the ancient world, particularly in societies like Greece, women had virtually no power outside the home. For all the vaunted democracy of Greece, women couldn't vote or even speak in public. Yet as prophetesses they were able to gain power that was denied to them everywhere else. We're going to hear about a lot of powerful women in this book.

A notable feature of Delphi was that while delivering a prophecy the priestess was supposed to be in a frenzied, semiconscious state. There was much speculation that volcanic fumes or some other sort of natural gas might seep into the temple, giving rise to both the legend of the Py-

A decorative, if not accurate, nineteenth-century view of the Pythia at Delphi. In actual fact, wrestling with snakes was not part of her prophetic procedure.

thon and the Pythia's entranced condition. A nice neat theory, but unfortunately modern excavations at Delphi have found absolutely nothing to support it. It's possible that the priestess inhaled smoke from hemp or some other substance that produces a narcotic smoke—but no one really knows. Delphi was visited and written about for centuries, yet its inner workings remain a mystery.

The setting at Delphi was spectacular. The temple complex was perched on a high crag and could be reached only after a long climb up a steep and difficult trail. After performing the proper rituals (and doubtless paying the proper fees), the pilgrim was allowed to ask a question. Usually the questions were written, and the answers were also delivered in writing. Only rarely was the questioner allowed within the sacred precincts of the shrine itself.

Inside the shrine sat the Pythia atop a tall golden tripod. The emotional effect of visiting a place like Delphi had to be overwhelming. But how accurate were the prophecies?

That was something that King Croesus of Lydia, who reigned from 560 to 546 B.C., wanted to know. There were a number of famous oracles in the world, all of which claimed 100 percent accuracy. Croesus decided to test them. This was history's first known test of prophecy. He sent ambassadors to each of the leading shrines. They were all to ask the same question: What is the king doing at home in Sardis, his capital, on the hundredth day after the ambassadors had left him?

On the one-hundredth day the king did the most unlikely thing he could think of. In secret he cut up a lamb and a tortoise and boiled their flesh in a bronze pot with a bronze lid. No one knew what he had done, and even if they had, there would have been no way to communicate the information to any of the oracles.

One by one the ambassadors returned with the oracles' answers to the king's question. All of the answers proved wide of the mark, except the one received from Delphi. It read:

I know the number of the sand, and all the measures of the sea. I understand the dumb, and hear the voice that speaketh not. A savor has assailed my nostrils of a strong shelled tortoise boiled with lamb's flesh in bronze, both laid beneath and set above.

That was a direct hit, and it convinced Croesus that Delphi was genuine. But the story does not end there.

Croesus was so impressed that he showered Delphi with gifts, which he could well afford to do for he was enormously wealthy. The phrase "rich as Croesus" is still used today to describe someone of vast wealth. Among the gifts was a gold bowl weighing a quarter of a ton.

The king regularly consulted the oracle on political matters affecting his kingdom. His greatest worry was the growing power of the Persians, a neighboring people. He sent a messenger to Delphi asking if he should end the threat by attacking the Persians first. The answer he got was:

When Croesus shall o'er Halys river go,
He will a mighty kingdom overthrow.

The Halys, a river in Asia Minor, separated the lands of Persia from Croesus's Lydia. Croesus, who had wanted to attack the Persians all along, took this answer as a sign that the oracle approved his plan. He attacked but was utterly defeated, and the Kingdom of Lydia was absorbed by the Persian Empire.

As you might imagine, the former king, who had poured so much treasure into Delphi, felt betrayed. He sent an angry message to the shrine. The answer he received, roughly translated, read, "You didn't ask which kingdom!"

We know for a fact that King Croesus was a generous patron of Delphi and that he was defeated by the Persians. How much of the rest of the story is fact and how much is legend we simply do not know. But the story does point out one great shortcoming with Delphi, indeed with almost all prophetic statements. They are couched in poetic, symbolic, or often just plain confusing language. They can be interpreted in a large number of very different ways. The term "Delphic reply" came to mean an answer that was ambiguous and difficult to understand. In the story Croesus decided that the oracle's answer endorsed what he wanted to do anyway. That is a situation that we will find repeated constantly throughout the history of prophecy.

The Pythia's answers were so frenzied and garbled that they had to be interpreted by priests who were specially appointed for the job. It was the priests' interpretation of the Pythia's prophecy that was presented, usually in poetic form, to the questioner. Thus another step was added between the original prophetic inspiration and the ultimate answer, another chance for misinterpretation, error and just plain fraud.

Throughout the oracle's long history there were frequent accusations that the priests had been bribed to give answers favorable to one side or another in a conflict. Like other seers in history, Delphi also had a particular political point of view (conservative and traditional), and this view was reflected in the pronouncements that came from the shrine.

There were human problems as well. Originally the Pythia was chosen from among the young virgins of the region. But the love affairs of these supposedly pure maidens became notorious. Finally, after one particularly attractive young Pythia was actually carried out of the shrine by her lover, those who controlled Delphi decided a change was needed. From then on the Pythias were picked from among elderly spinsters.

Delphi was not the only oracle in Greece. The most ancient oracle in Greece was at Dodona, a mountainous region in the northwestern part of the country. For a thousand years before the Greeks attained their high civilization, people gathered around a sacred oak to see if they could hear in the rustling of its leaves a message from the god Zeus. In later time the process of consulting the oracle became formalized. The branches of the oak were hung with bronze bowls, and a group of priests was appointed to interpret the rustling of the leaves, the cooing of the doves, the babbling of a nearby brook, and the clashing of the bowls. These sounds were believed to be the voice of Zeus.

Visiting the oracle at Labadeia was a fatiguing experience. After spending several days performing sacrifices and purification rites, the pilgrim entered a pit and crawled through a narrow passage into a dark cavern where the god spoke to him. The experience was usually so terrifying that once the pilgrim emerged into the light, he could not remember what the god had told him until the priests led him to the Seat of Memory and helped him to remember what he had heard.

Outside Greece the most celebrated oracle was the shrine of the god Amen-Ra located deep in the Egyptian desert. When Alexander the Great conquered Egypt in 332 B.C., he made a famous visit to the shrine. Accompanied only by a few close companions, the conqueror made the dangerous trek across the desert to the shrine. What question he asked, and what answer he received, is unknown. But after his visit Alexander began to insist that he be given divine honors. The rumor spread that the oracle told him he was the direct descendant of the god Amen-Ra.

Earlier in his career Alexander had a less satisfying experience at Delphi. He arrived on a day when the Pythia did not prophesy. Not to be thwarted, the conqueror grabbed the priestess and dragged her toward the tripod from which she issued her pronouncements. The poor woman gasped, "My lad, you are invincible." That answer was good enough for Alexander.

Not everyone believed in the value of oracles. The Greek philosophers were skeptical of many things, including oracles, even though Delphi had once pronounced the philosopher Socrates "the wisest man in the world." Ultimately the oracles began to lose their hold on the common folk as well. By the first century of the Christian era, the great oracle at Delphi got along with a single Pythia, whereas in earlier days at least three Pythias were kept busy at a time.

People did a lot of speculating on the reasons for the decline in oracles. The Greek writer Putarch (A.D. 46–120) even wrote a book on the subject. One reason advanced was that the gods, disgusted with human wickedness, had stopped answering questions. Another was that there existed a natural cycle that controlled the spirits that activated oracles and that the spirits had gone away but would return someday.

Perhaps the most haunting and enigmatic story about

the decline of oracles was told by a sailor who, while cruising the coast near Epirus, heard a voice from the shore calling, "When you come to Palodes, announce that the Great Pan is dead!" The death of the woodland god was supposed to mark the beginning of the decline of oracles.

Whatever the reasons for the decline, the practice of consulting oracles lingered in the Roman world until the triumph of Christianity. The Christian emperors either discouraged or actively persecuted the remaining oracular shrines. Delphi predicted its own demise. Constantine, the first Christian emperor, stole the sacred tripod from the shrine and carried it off to Constantinople (now Istanbul), where it remains to this day. Priests and patrons of oracles were often tortured and killed.

Christianity brought an end to the age of the oracle, but a few ancient beliefs and practices remained, particularly in Greece. There were churches that issued prophecies much as the pagan oracles had. As late as 1920, priests at the Church of Saint George Balsamites on the island of Amorgos dipped water from a prophetic stream and divined the future from the debris found floating in the water.

And the people at Delphi still make their living off the shrine, though now it is simply a popular tourist attraction, not a place of prophecy.

OMENS AND PORTENTS

4

History is full of cautionary tales of what happened to those who were foolhardy enough to ignore prophetic warnings. On the eve of an important sea battle with the Carthaginians, the Roman admiral Claudius Pulcher received some bad news. The sacred chickens had stopped eating. That was considered a very unfavorable omen. Claudius was more irritated than frightened. "Throw the blasted chickens into the sea," he shouted. "If they won't eat, let them drink." The Romans then sailed into battle and were badly defeated.

There is not a lot of historical evidence to support this little story, but it just might be true. A lot of Romans certainly believed it. While the Greeks had their oracles, the ancient Romans relied on the interpretation of omens and portents. An omen is any unusual event that seems to fore-shadow an important change in human affairs. A portent is a particularly strong omen.

The Romans were not the only people in history to look to omens. The course of Greek history may actually have been altered by the interpretation of that most spectacular of omens—an eclipse. In 415 B.C. the Athenians launched an expedition against the island of Syracuse. The expedition fared badly and was ready to retreat when a lunar eclipse occurred. The Athenian commander Nicias decided that was a bad omen, and he delayed his departure. As a result, Nicias was attacked and lost his fleet, his soldiers, and his own life.

There was no set way of interpreting an omen such as an eclipse. It usually meant bad luck, but for whom? When Alexander the Great observed a lunar eclipse on the eve of a particular battle, he told his men it was a bad omen for the enemy. The next day he attacked and won.

The Romans did not like to leave the interpretation of omens to amateurs. The state employed a special body of men called augurs whose duty it was to interpret eclipses, thunder, the behavior of birds and animals, or any unusual events. The historian Livy listed hundreds of portents that supposedly occurred at the time of Hannibal's invasion of Italy:

A six-months-old child, of freeborn parents, is said to have shouted "Io triumphe" in the vegetable market, whilst in the Forum Bearum, an ox is reported to have climbed up of its own accord to the third story of a house, and then, frightened by the noisy crowd that gathered, it threw itself down. A phantom navy was seen shining in the sky; the temple of Hope in the veg-

etable market was struck by lightning; at Lanvium, Juno's spear had moved itself, and a crow had flown down to the temple and settled on her couch; in the territory of Amiternum beings in human shape and clothed in white were seen at a distance, but no one came close to them.

You might just find accounts very similar to these in the pages of some of today's supermarket tabloids. Livy himself was rather skeptical of such reports and thought they might be the result of "superstitious fear."

That is the other side of the story, for like Claudius Pulcher, a lot of Romans were skeptical of omens. The sharp-tongued politician Cato snapped, "I wonder a soothsayer doesn't laugh when he sees another soothsayer."

Roman leaders often cynically exploited the people's beliefs in omens by interpreting them to suit their own purposes. Julius Caesar was probably as skeptical as anyone who has lived. Yet he was able to bribe his way into the position of Rome's chief religious officer, a position he used to further his own political and military career.

When he came to Africa to conduct a campaign against his enemy Pompey the Great, Caesar tripped and fell on his face when getting off the ship. His soldiers were horrified, for this terrible omen surely signified that Caesar's cause, like Caesar himself, would fall. Caesar recognized the danger. He jumped up from the ground and shouted, "Africa, I embrace you!"—thus completely reversing the traditional meaning of the omen. The soldiers cheered and marched off to a quick victory.

Caesar's life, however, contains one of history's most celebrated tales of the folly of ignoring prophetic advice. A soothsayer was said to have warned the Roman leader to

*Roman augurs illustrating Cato's cynical remark,
"I wonder a soothsayer doesn't laugh when he
sees another soothsayer."*

"beware the Ides of March"—March 15. Caesar paid no heed and went to the Senate unprotected by his usual bodyguard on March 15. There he was stabbed to death by a group of conspirators.

Was Caesar a fool for ignoring the warning? If one thing was characteristic of Caesar's life, it was his boldness. In the tumultuous and violent world of Roman politics Caesar had often faced the possibilities of assassination and execution. As a general he shared his soldiers' hardships and dangers. He must have been warned hundreds of times that his life was in peril. He ignored the warnings, which, up to the moment he was stabbed, had been extraordinary.

It's too easy to dismiss as ignorant and primitive all those Romans who did believe in the predictive powers of omens. The Romans were a highly civilized and very practical people. A belief in omens is supported by a more general belief that nothing happens by accident, that everything in the natural world is connected in some way with everything else, that everything has a meaning if only that meaning could be properly interpreted.

The Romans and the Greeks before them developed a whole philosophical system to account for omens. The doctrine was called *sympathism*. It holds that all parts of the universe are interconnected by powerful but unknown forces. There is no space in such a universe for random or chance events. The universe is a whole, a great and perfect design. Around the year A.D. 400, a man named Synesios carried the doctrine of sympathism to its logical extreme. Noting that the Romans had often tried to predict the future by observing the movement of birds, he concluded that birds, if they had the intelligence, could actually predict the future by observing the movements of humans!

There was also the belief that the gods could reveal themselves in many different ways. And that helps to explain what most people now consider to be the strangest and messiest method of divining the future: *haruspicy*, or predicting the future by examining the entrails of sacrificed animals.

Haruspicy was an extremely ancient and widespread practice. It dated at least from the time of the ancient Babylonians. The Romans inherited the practice from the Etruscans, who had once ruled Rome. Rather than dying out, it gained a larger following as Rome grew more powerful. In time the haruspices succeeded the augurs as the leading official government diviners. In one form or another, this practice can be found throughout the world, in places far removed from Babylon or Rome.

Like many other ancient practices, this one has a certain strange logic behind it. When an animal was sacrificed to a god, it was believed that the animal was absorbed by the god to whom the sacrifice had been offered. This created a direct channel to that god. By opening the carcass, the haruspex might be able to get a glimpse at any message the god left inside the offering.

It was the examination of the liver of a sacrificed bull that led the haruspex Spurinna Vestricus to warn his patron Julius Caesar to watch out for his life on the Ides of March.

Today we no longer examine bulls' livers to try to discover what the future holds. But practically all of us retain at least a subconscious belief in omens. Black cats, broken mirrors, and spilled salt are still regarded, if only half seriously, as harbingers of bad luck. Four-leaf clovers are signs of good luck. Break a shoelace first thing in the morning and you're likely to think that you're going to have a bad day. And earthquakes, epidemics, and wars are seen as portents of even more catastrophic events to come.

THE PUZZLE OF PROPHECY

5

The myths and legends of history present prophets as a strange and often tragic lot. "The gift of prophecy," it seems, was not an unmixed blessing.

According to Greek mythology, Cassandra, daughter of King Priam of Troy, was given the gift of prophecy by the god Apollo. In return she was supposed to love him, but she didn't. So Apollo took his revenge. He asked Cassandra for a single kiss, and when his lips touched hers, he withdrew her powers of persuasion. Thus Cassandra could still foretell the future, but no one ever believed her. Because she was always saying gloomy and unpopular things, she was hated and ultimately murdered. Cassandra foresaw her own murder, of course, but was powerless to prevent it.

Another prophet in Greek mythology was Tiresias, the blind seer of Thebes. According to the myths, Tiresias had once been asked to settle an argument between the god Zeus and his wife Hera. When Tiresias said that Zeus had the better argument, the enraged Hera blinded him. Zeus responded by giving him long life and the gift of prophecy.

Merlin, from the medieval King Arthur legends, was commonly called a magician, but he was also a prophet. The original Merlin stories may well go back to pre-Christian times. When Merlin was incorporated into the Arthurian legends, which were Christian, this created problems. Merlin was a magician, not a saint. Since his powers clearly did not come from God, they were attributed to the Devil. The first written account of Merlin's birth appears in a French book printed in Paris in 1498. The book states that Merlin spoke the instant he was born. Merlin's first prophecy was to assure his mother, a virtuous young woman, that she would not die in childbirth, as many of her unfriendly neighbors had predicted. A judge in the district heard of the marvelous event and summoned both mother and child to appear before him. This they did, and in order to test the baby prophet the judge asked him if he knew his own father, to which the infant Merlin replied in a clear voice, "Yes, my father is the Devil; and I have his power and know all things past, present and to come." The judge prudently decided that this terrifying child should not be molested in any way.

Many prophecies were attributed to Merlin, but all the best ones were written up long after the prophesied event had already occurred. A book called *History of the Britons*, written about the year 800, contains some of Merlin's alleged prophecies. These are completely accurate up to the time the book was written. For events beyond the time the book was written, Merlin's prophecies are not much good. For example, the author has Merlin predicting the eventual reconquest of the British Isles by the native Britons. A war between the Britons and the invading Saxons was still dragging on at that time, and there was a chance, though a slim one, that the Britons might be victorious. By the twelfth century, however, another author had Merlin foreseeing the ultimate defeat of the Britons, since by that time the Britons had virtually ceased to exist as a separate people.

Even for the great Merlin, however, "the gift of prophecy" seems to have availed little. He foresaw that the wicked Nimue would eventually bring about his destruction. Yet he calmly continued his love affair with her, as though he knew nothing of his coming fate.

Cassandra, Tiresias, and Merlin are all prophets of myth and legend. While their stories have been told and retold in some of the most famous and widely read literature in history, it's doubtful that their prophecies ever really influenced the way people acted. The Sibyls are quite a different matter. There may once have been a group of seeresses living in Italy on whom the stories of the Sibyls are based. By the time people began writing about them, the history of the Sibyls had already become hopelessly confused.

We do know this much—there were books of prophecy attributed to the Sibyls that were held in awe by the Romans. The Sibyls were so popular in Rome that even when the Roman Empire became Christianized, many people continued to believe in the prophecies of the Sibyls. In Christian times the Sibyls were often accorded a position in literature and art almost at a level with that of the

Old Testament prophets. The artist Michelangelo painted the Sibyls in the Sistine Chapel in Rome.

Of these prophetesses the best known is the Cumaean Sibyl, who was said to live in a cave near the modern city of Naples. You can still see the cave, or more accurately, a whole mass of caves and tunnels at the site of the ancient town of Cumae, about 6 miles (9 kilometers) west of Naples.

The legends say that the Cumaean Sibyl was granted one wish by the god Apollo. She asked to live for as many years as there were grains of sand in her hand. But she failed

The Sibyl of Cumae as painted by Michelangelo in the Sistine Chapel in Rome. There are those who believe she still resides in a cave near Naples.

to ask for eternal youth as well, so she became extremely aged and decrepit. As is usual, the prophet or prophetess is unable to avoid a fate that should have been foreseen.

Like so many other prophetic utterances, the prophecies of the Cumaean Sibyl were extremely confusing and hard to decipher. It was said that she had written her prophecies on palm leaves, but that the wind had scattered the leaves; when they were gathered up, they could never again be arranged in the proper order.

These prophecies were supposed to contain the entire future history of Rome and the Latin race. One particularly interesting story relates how there were originally nine Sibylline books of Roman history. These the prophetess offered, at a very high price, to Tarquinius the Proud, the last king of Rome (534–510 B.C.). Living up to his name, Tarquinius was too proud to pay the price at first, whereupon the prophetess cast three of the books into the fire and offered the remaining six at the same price. Tarquinius was shocked, but he still refused, so the Sibyl put three more of the precious volumes in the flames and offered the remaining three with no reduction in price. This time Tarquinius the Proud paid.

There very probably was a real prophetess or group of prophetesses whose sayings and deeds inspired the legend of the Sibyls. But their authentic history is lost. Whether this theoretical individual or group also composed the Sibylline books is an open question. Tradition says that the books kept at Rome were the very ones that Tarquinius purchased from the Cumaean Sibyl.

Whatever their origin, the Sibylline books were considered great treasures and were stored beneath the Capitol in Rome. They could be read only by a special body of fifteen priests in times of national emergency, and then only at the command of the Senate. The original set of Sibylline books is believed to have been destroyed when the Capitol was burned in 83 B.C., but a new collection was then put together from various sources. The Sibylline books were last officially consulted in A.D. 363.

According to the laws of Rome, access to the Sibylline books was severely restricted—death was the stated penalty for an unauthorized look at the precious volumes. Yet many copies of the books turned up in the hands of wealthy private citizens. The last complete copy of the books is believed to have been burned by Flavius Stulicho, a German mercenary who controlled the Western Roman Empire in the early fifth century.

Still, fragments of Sibylline prophecy, or what is said to be Sibylline prophecy, survive. Little, if any, of this material dates from the original books kept at Rome. Much of it was compiled or composed by the Jewish community of Alexandria in Egypt. It was a common practice throughout the ancient world to attribute original works to earlier and more famous sources. Here is a typical prophecy from these "Sibylline books":

The Kingdom of God shall come upon good Men; for the Earth which is the producer of all things, shall yield to Men the best, and infinite Fruits . . . and the Cities shall be full of good Men, and the Fields shall be fruitful, and there shall be no war in the Earth, nor Tumult, nor shall the Earth groan by an Earthquake, nor Wars, nor Drought, nor Famine, nor Hail

*to waste the Fruits; but there shall be great Peace in all
the Earth and one King shall live in Friendship with
the other, to the End of the Age.*

This glowingly optimistic forecast goes on to predict the
rise of Judaism to the world religion, and an era of perfect
justice. Quite obviously the prophecy has not been fulfilled.
Such a "prophecy" really reflected the hopes of those who
composed it. Later, Christians produced similar "Sibylline
prophecies" that told of the Second Coming of Christ and
the ultimate, worldwide triumph of Christianity.

There have been prophets and prophetesses in every
age. Some attain only temporary fame. Others catch the
public imagination and become the stuff of legends.

The celebrated English seeress known as Mother
Shipton was said to have been born in Yorkshire around
1488 and to have lived there until her death in 1561. Her
maiden name was reported to have been Ursula Southill.
At the age of about twenty-four, she married a carpenter
named Toby Shipton and settled in a small village just north
of York. She was described as a large and extremely ugly—
but very pious—woman.

The prophetess lived through the reign of Henry VIII
and was reported to have predicted the downfall and death
of many powerful persons during that turbulent era. There
have been numerous retellings of her prediction of the arrest of the king's most influential minister, Cardinal Wolsey.
Here is one account:

> *When Cardinal Wolsey intended to remove his resi-
> dence to York she announced that he would never reach
> the city. The Cardinal sent three lords of his retinue in*

Mother Shipton met Cardinal Wolsey, but when?

*disguise to inquire whether she had made such a pre-diction, and to threaten her if she persisted in it. . . .
The retainers, led by a guide named Beasly, knocked
at the door.*

*"Come in, Mr. Beasly, and three noble lords with
you," said Mother Shipton.*

*She treated them civilly, by setting oat cakes and
ale before them.*

*"You gave out," said they, "the Cardinal should
never see York."*

*"No," she replied, "I said that he might see it, but
never come to it."*

*They responded: "When he does come he'll surely
burn thee."*

"If this burn," said the Reverend Mother, "so shall I."

She then cast her linen handkerchief into the fire, allowed it to remain in the flames a quarter of an hour, and took it out unsinged.

[Burning, incidentally, was no idle threat to prophets in Henry VIII's day. Henry burned several who had issued prophecies that hinted at his failure in some enterprise.]

One of her awe-stricken visitors then asked what she thought of him.

She answered, "The time will come, lord, when you shall be as low as I am, and that is low indeed."

[The questioner in this case was Thomas Lord Cromwell, Wolsey's supporter, and later his successor. Cromwell ultimately fell from favor and was beheaded by the King.]

Cardinal Wolsey, on his arrival at Cawood, ascended the castle tower, and while viewing York, 8 miles (12 kilometers) off, vowed he would burn the witch when he reached there. But ere he descended the stairs, a message from the King demanded his presence forthwith and while on his journey to London he was taken ill and died at Leicester.

Such a prophecy would have been quite remarkable if it had been made in 1530, the date attributed to it. But the earliest account of the prophecy—indeed, the earliest written account of Mother Shipton—appears in a pamphlet issued in 1641, when the predicted event had already taken place.

In the years following 1641, the body of Shiptonian legend and prophecy grew enormously. New prophecies were always being "discovered." A play called *The Life and Death of Mother Shipton* appeared in 1684. Here Mother Shipton, like Merlin before her, is described as an offspring of the Devil.

The most complete "life" of Mother Shipton, and the one from which most of the stories of her prophecies are taken, was written by S. Baker and published in 1794. According to Baker, Mother Shipton correctly foretold the hour of her own death and succumbed "with much serenity, A.D. 1571, when upwards of seventy years of age." Between the villages of Clifton and Skipton a monument was said to have been erected to her bearing this epitaph:

Here ly's she who never ly'd,
Whose skill often has been try'd
Her prophecies shall survive,
And ever keep her name alive.

Unfortunately, this interesting monument, if it ever existed, perished long ago.

The most uncanny of all the Shipton prophecies was a fifty-seven-line bit of doggerel verse. It was said to have first appeared in print in 1447 and was republished in 1641. Since Mother Shipton was supposed to have been born in 1488, some forty years after the prophecy was first published, there are some obvious problems with dates. In fact, the celebrated rhyme first appeared in a book of Shiptonian prophecy edited by Charles Hindley in 1862. At that time the poem created quite a bit of excitement. From the following extract you can see why:

Carriages without horses shall go,
And accidents fill the world with woe . . .
Around the world thought shall fly
In the twinkling of an eye . . .
Through the hills men shall ride
And no horse or ass by their side,
Under water men shall walk,
Shall ride, shall sleep, shall talk.
In the air men shall be seen
In white, in black, in green;
Iron in the water shall float,
As easily as a wooden boat . . .
Fire and water shall wonders do,
England shall at last admit a foe.
The world to an end shall come
In eighteen hundred and eighty one.

The prophecy was clearly wrong about the date the world would end. It was also wrong about England being successfully invaded. But the rest of the prophecies are utterly sensational if they were actually made by a sixteenth-century countrywoman. But the truth is quite unsensational. The verses were composed by Hindley himself, shortly before he published his book of Mother Shipton's prophecies. Hindley later admitted to the forgery. Though Hindley seems to have made a rather shrewd guess about the large number of auto accidents that were to accompany the popularity of the "horseless carriage," his other predictions were not that astonishing for someone living in the mid-nineteenth century.

Few take Mother Shipton seriously today. Merlin is generally regarded as a completely legendary character, and the Sibylline books are no longer consulted by anyone. But there is a prophet of a past age who still commands a large and serious following today. And he deserves a chapter of his own.

NOSTRADAMUS

6

The predictions of a sixteenth-century French prophet are still fascinating and frightening people of the late twentieth century. The prophet is Michel de Notredame (1503–66), better known as Nostradamus. His celebrated book of prophecies called *Centuries*, first published in 1555, has interested many and obsessed others ever since. Today, his enigmatic prophecies, some of which seem to predict the end of the world by about the year 2000, are more popular and influential than they have been for a long time.

In order to understand the Nostradamus phenomenon, we must first know something of the man and his time. Unlike many prophets of past ages whose histories are unknown or completely legendary, a good deal is known about Nostradamus.

He was born on December 14, 1503, at Saint-Remy in Provence, France. His parents were prosperous and educated Jews who had converted to Christianity—whether they did so of their own free will or because they felt forced to is unclear. Nostradamus was a bright and attentive lad and was given a good education. Though he studied astrology, as did most of the other educated men of his day, he showed no particular interest in prophecy while young.

In 1525 he obtained a medical degree and spent the next four years as an itinerant healer in the south of France. At the town of Agen he married a woman said to be "of high estate, very beautiful and very amiable," though her name has been lost. She bore him a son and a daughter.

There were recurrent outbreaks of plague, and treating its victims made up a good part of the young doctor's practice. His remedies were fairly conventional, though he did refuse to bleed his patients. Bleeding was a common medical treatment of the day; it hurt many patients and helped absolutely none. For that reason alone Nostradamus was probably a better doctor than most of his contemporaries.

In 1538 his wife and children died in an outbreak of plague. Patients suddenly became very wary of a doctor who could not save his own family. His wife's family sued for the return of her dowry. Nostradamus also came under the suspicious eye of the Inquisition, not for issuing prophecies—that phase of his career had yet to begin—but for allegedly making a slighting remark about a statue of the Virgin. He was ordered to appear before the Inquisitor at Toulouse. Rather than face what would have been at best an unpleasant and quite possibly a dangerous experience, he took to the road. From 1538 to 1544 he again wandered about as an itinerant physician, mostly in southern France.

It was during this six-year period of wandering that he first seems to have developed a deep interest in astrology and prophecy in general. A number of quite unverifiable stories of his prophetic powers date from this time.

Typical is an account of his meeting with a humble Franciscan monk while traveling in Italy. He bowed down before the astonished cleric and addressed him as "Your Holiness." Years after the seer's death the monk, by that time a cardinal, was elected Pope Sixtus V.

Finally Nostradamus settled in the little town of Salon, where he married Anne Ponsarde Gemelle, a rich widow. At Salon, Nostradamus was engaged primarily in the practice of making cosmetics for the rich. This seems a harmless enough activity, but he was not a universally popular fellow. The mid-sixteenth century was a time of fierce religious hatreds and a paralyzing fear of witchcraft and sorcery. Nostradamus, a descendant of converted Jews and a suspected Huguenot sympathizer, faced enormous hostility. The Huguenots were the Protestants of predominantly Catholic France. His interest in occult studies, which developed during his wandering years, did nothing to improve his reputation among his neighbors. Nostradamus retired more and more from those around him, whom he denounced as "barbarians," and he plunged ever deeper into his study and practice of the occult.

By 1550 he appears to have become fully committed to the prophecy business and had issued his first almanac. Almanacs filled with prophecies for the coming year were popular in those days, just as astrology magazines are today. Nostradamus soon built a substantial reputation as a compiler of almanacs.

Nostradamus, from the frontispiece to a collection of his prophecies published in 1666.

If that were all Nostradamus had ever done, he would be as forgotten as a host of other sixteenth-century almanac compilers. But he undertook a far more ambitious project. He wrote prophetic verses, each containing four lines (quatrains). These were arranged in ten books of one hundred verses each, called the *Centuries*. Actually, one of the books contains only 42 verses, and the total number of verses is 942, not 1,000, as might be expected. Why the prophet did not produce a round number of prophecies is unknown. The *Centuries* were to contain prophecies for the next two thousand years, or specifically until the year 3797. The first edition appeared in 1555 but contained only three of the ten books and part of the fourth. Complete editions were not in print until 1557. It is this work on which Nostradamus's fame is based.

Before we look at the content of the *Centuries*, we can speculate for a moment on Nostradamus's method of prophecy—but we can only speculate, for he never laid down a formula. According to some later accounts the seer, dressed in full magical regalia, would retire to his secret study and after performing the proper rituals, would gaze into a bowl of water and see visions of the future. This sort of "scrying," as it is called, was a common enough practice among occultists, but there is no hard evidence that Nostradamus ever employed such techniques. He was an astrologer, and there are many indications of astrological influence in his prophecies. Like other educated men of his day he was well versed in the Bible, and his prophecies contain recurring echoes of biblical prophecy as well.

He said that his work was to be "a memorial of me after my death, to the common benefit of mankind, concerning the thing which the Divine Essence has revealed to me by astronomical revelations."

The language of the *Centuries* is extremely obscure. Nostradamus wrote in a Latinized French that was archaic, even in his day. He often employed puns and anagrams or simply made up words and phrases. Nostradamus was unapologetic about the obscurity of his predictions. He didn't want to directly offend the Church or other powerful forces. If he did, they might condemn not only the prophecies, but the prophet himself. He wrote: "If I came to refer to that which will be in the future, those of realm, sect, religion, and faith would find it so poorly in accord with their petty fancies that they would come to condemn."

In addition to the confusion caused by the obscure language, Nostradamus rarely put dates on his predictions, and the *Centuries* are not in chronological order. A quatrain in the First Century might refer to an event that was to take place hundreds of years later, whereas a quatrain in a later Century might describe an event that was to occur within Nostradamus's own lifetime.

It's easy to understand why prophets, eager to protect their own skin, would be obscure about events that were close at hand. It's not as easy to understand why Nostradamus couldn't be more specific about events that were to take place long after his death. How could such predictions be "to the common benefit of mankind," if mankind could not make head nor tail of them?

The *Centuries* received a mixed reaction from the public. Doctors and astrologers accused the seer of dishonoring their professions, while philosophers objected to his premises. Most enraged of all were the poets who decried the miserable quality of his verse. Even Nostradamus's most devoted and uncritical admirers are unable to defend his merits as a poet.

But Nostradamus had his supporters, most notably in the court of King Henry II, where the *Centuries* were all the rage. They were particularly popular with Queen Catherine de Médicis, a great patron of astrologers and magicians. Catherine was said to have asked Nostradamus to forecast the future of her children. Exactly what happened we do not know; according to one sensational account, Nostradamus conjured up the angel Anael who showed Catherine the future of her children in a mirror.

Nostradamus showing Queen Catherine the future monarchs of France in his "magic mirror."

Three of her sons were to become kings, but their reigns were to be both brief and tragic. These sons paraded across the mirror once for every year of their reign. The parade did not take long. Then Catherine's hated son-in-law Henry, king of Navarre, who was later to succeed to the French throne as Henry IV, appeared in the mirror and took twenty-three turns. When his descendants—who were to remain kings of France until the Revolution—began appearing, Catherine became so depressed that she called off the session.

The mirror scene is dramatic, but unlikely. More probably the prophet simply cast horoscopes for the royal children. Even if the cautious Nostradamus did possess the ability to see the future, it is extremely unlikely that he would have given the queen such a bleak forecast. Monarchs were not fond of prophets who brought them bad news. Those who predicted disaster for royalty were often suspected of wishing for or plotting such a disaster. As we have already seen, Nostradamus, who knew that his position was precarious, was an extremely careful man who made his prophecies so difficult to interpret that they could not be turned against him. He may simply have predicted that Catherine's sons would become kings, which was true enough as far as it went.

However, Nostradamus's most celebrated prophecy apparently was concerned with what was to befall King Henry II himself. This famous quatrain, which is in stanza 35 of the First Century, illustrates some of the difficulties encountered when trying to interpret the *Centuries*. It reads:

> *The young lion will overcome the old one*
> *On the field of battle in a single combat:*
> *He will put out his eyes in a cage of gold:*
> *Two fleets one, then to die a cruel death.*

On July 1, 1559, King Henry was riding in a tournament against Gabriel de Lorges, Comte de Montgomery, captain of the Spanish Guard. The lances of the two riders met and splintered. Montgomery dropped his shaft a second too late, and the jagged point pierced the visor of the king's helmet and entered his left eye. Henry fell from the saddle and died in agony some ten days later.

That prediction looks close to the mark, so close, in fact, that it got the prophet in trouble. According to a biography of Nostradamus written by his son Caesar, the common folk confused prophecy with a curse and burned the prophet in effigy, and the Church considered burning the prophet himself. But the powerful queen remained his friend, and he was in no real danger.

Nostradamus became an honored man and a wealthy one. While he was often denounced, just as often he was consulted by leading figures in France, particularly the queen, and by nobles from other countries as well.

Nostradamus is said to have predicted that he would die in November 1567. In fact, he died over a year earlier, in July 1566. According to another story, when he fell ill he told a friend at his bedside, "You will not find me alive at sunrise." True to form, at least in this account, he died that very night. In his will Nostradamus expressed the curious wish to be buried standing upright, supposedly so that the boorish people of Salon would not step on his body.

Many of the stories about Nostradamus, like the one about predicting the fate of the children of Catherine de Médicis, must be dismissed for lack of credible evidence. His almanacs, in which he made short-term and relatively specific predictions, are no better than the almanacs compiled by hundreds of others who preceded and followed him. His reputation must rise or fall on the *Centuries*.

Now let's return to the quatrain that apparently predicts the cruel death of King Henry II. Neither the name of the king nor that of the man who killed him is given. They are described as the young lion and the old one. In fact, the king was only forty, a mere six years older than the man who accidentally killed him. A tournament field is not a field of battle. While the visor of a helmet may resemble a cage, the king's helmet was not gilded. The reference to two "fleets" is both obscure and controversial. The original word is *classes*, which some have translated as fractures or wounds. It is not unreasonable to assume that in the accident the king received two wounds. But Nostradamus also used the word *classes* to signify fleets of ships, so the meaning is unclear. Such arguments might be dismissed as nit-picking quibbles. But this quatrain is considered the clearest and best of the seer's predictions.

Nostradamus enthusiasts point to another possible reference to the death of Henry II. It comes in the 55th stanza of the Third Century. Here the seer speaks of a "one-eyed man" ruling France. In the ten days between the king's accident and his death, he may well have been a "one-eyed man," the only one ever to rule France, however briefly. But if he is said to have his "eyes" put out in the first quatrain, how can he become a "one-eyed man" in the second? Another quibble, but they add up.

More confusion comes from apparent references to Henry II in other quatrains, which appear to predict a bright future for the king. If it turned out that Henry II had a long and prosperous reign, these could be cited as fulfilled predictions. In hindsight they are ignored or reinterpreted.

The interpreters of Nostradamus have been extremely clever at relating his quatrains to an event—after that event has taken place. When they have tried to use Nostradamus as a guide to times beyond when the interpretations are made, the only true test of prophecy, they have slipped badly. As usual, the interpreters came up with predictions that suited their own purposes.

Those interested in Nostradamus who were also followers of Napoleon found in the *Centuries* predictions that Napoleon would conquer England and have a long and peaceful reign. They were wrong.

Followers of Nostradamus who were also supporters of the French monarchy during Napoleon's time correctly predicted the restoration of the House of Bourbon. However, the restoration was brief, and they kept right on predicting the return of the Bourbons throughout the nineteenth century. Some may still be looking for the rise of a new king of France.

During World War I, French Nostradamians found that the master had predicted a victory for France, while their German counterparts saw German victory clearly written in the *Centuries*. During World War II, both German and Allied intelligence agencies produced interpretations of the quatrains that were supposed to predict victory for their respective sides. These were distributed as propaganda intended to demoralize the enemy but apparently had no effect.

Aside from propaganda, many followers of Nostradamus say that he clearly predicted the rise of Hitler and the outbreak of World War II. In the *Centuries* there are numerous references to "Hister," a name some interpret as Hitler. In fact, "Hister" was a Latin word for the river we call the Danube in central Europe, which would have been well known to Nostradamus. There is even a reference to a bridge over the Hister.

Nostradamus has been credited with predicting the French Revolution, communism, nuclear warfare, the foundation of the state of Israel, Watergate, the AIDS epidemic, and even the 1991 war in the Persian Gulf. There are references to the rise of a tyrant in the ancient land of Mesopotamia, now Iraq. But the tyrant in the *Centuries* was notable for wearing a blue turban. This was not part of Saddam Hussein's collection of headgear. Predicting the rise of tyrants in the Middle East was a fairly safe bet, even in Nostradamus's time.

While Nostradamus has never really gone out of fashion, in recent years his works have enjoyed a renewed burst of popularity. That is because parts of the *Centuries* apparently can be interpreted to predict the end of the world as we know it, or at least some sort of cataclysmic event, at the end of the century and the millenium—around the year 2000. Thus the sixteenth-century seer appears to support the predictions of many other prophets, both ancient and modern.

Nostradamus doesn't actually come out and say the world will end in 1999; in fact, it is clear that he expects the world to continue in some form. But what he does say sends chills through those who believe in prophecies:

In the year 1999 and seven months—
From the sky will come the great King of Terror
He will raise to life the great King of the Mongols
Before and after war reign happily.

There are other references that apparently point to cataclysmic events at the end of the century, but his is the clearest, and it is one of the very rare predictions in which he actually uses a date. Did Nostradamus, peering into his bowl of water or poring over his astrological charts hundreds of years ago, somehow receive information about what will happen in the next few years of our lives? Well, perhaps. But predictions about cataclysms at the end of the second millennium of the Christian era would not have been surprising to Nostradamus's contemporaries.

In the sixteenth century it was assumed that the world was not very old, that it had begun somewhere around 4000 B.C. Bishop Ussher set the date at 4004 B.C. A popular view of the time was that the world as we know it would last about 6,000 years, which would bring us up to about the year 2000. Thus, rather than stating an original prophetic insight, Nostradamus may simply have been repeating a well-established traditional belief. Those who interpret the works of the French seer have a variety of candidates for "the Great King of Terror" and "the great King of the Mongols." There is no agreement on the meaning of the rest of the quatrain, but it sounds important.

There is one safe prediction that can be made. Even if the year 2000 comes and goes with no more than the usual number of disasters, the devoted followers of Nostradamus, forgetting all the current excitement about the end of the world, will claim that the master predicted it exactly, and they will continue to interpret and reinterpret the *Centuries* and find yet another date for doomsday.

THE SLEEPING PROPHET AND OTHERS

7

The modern era has had its share of prophets. One who has captured more than momentary fame is Edgar Cayce, often called "the sleeping prophet." He was so influential that years after his death an interpretation of some of his predictions set off a modest end-of-the-world panic.

Cayce was not one of those magical types who put on robes and gazed into bowls of water. He didn't even consult astrology charts. He got into prophecy through the back door, and his career is a uniquely American one.

There are a lot of different stories told about Cayce's development as a prophet, but this much seems certain. He was born in rural Kentucky in 1877, into a strongly religious family. As a boy and young man, Cayce appears to have held thoroughly conventional religious views and spent a lot of time reading the Bible. However, he didn't spend many years in school and apparently didn't get a great deal out of the time he was in the classroom. Even Cayce's most fervent admirers refer to him as "simple" and "unlettered." One of the great defenses of the prophet is that he was so uneducated that he couldn't possibly have made up all of the things he later talked about. After he left school, he tried a number of jobs and seemed to gain some success as a small-town photographer.

Then in 1900, Cayce inexplicably lost his voice and could not talk above a raspy whisper. He tried all the available remedies, but nothing seemed to work. He turned to the then-fashionable practice of Mesmerism. The name comes from Franz Anton Mesmer, an eighteenth-century Austrian physician who claimed that he could cure people by putting them into a trance. Mesmer's technique caught on throughout Europe and spread to America. It was refined and later became known as hypnotism. Mesmeric or hypnotic healers were familiar figures in nineteenth-century and early-twentieth-century America.

A local hypnotist, Al C. Layne, put Cayce into a trance. While entranced, the young man diagnosed his own condition as being psychological, and he cured himself.

This is not as amazing as it appears. Since ancient times there has been a belief that a sick person could go to sleep, and a god, or some other force, would reveal a cure to the person in his or her sleep. During the nineteenth century, hypnotists would put subjects into a trance and use an updated version of the old sleeping cure. In the case of psychologically based ailments such cures could work. Cayce's loss of voice was clearly such a condition.

Edgar Cayce was known as "the sleeping prophet" because of his ability to make predictions while in a self-induced trance.

Cayce was an excellent hypnotic subject and soon had developed a technique for putting himself into a trance. While entranced or "sleeping," he began diagnosing and prescribing for friends and neighbors. Once his reputation spread, he was able to give up photography and operate full-time as a "psychic healer." Technically he was not really a healer: he would diagnose a condition and then suggest a cure. He has been more accurately referred to as a "medical clairvoyant." There were a number of others who claimed similar powers, but Cayce quickly became the most famous. Usually the cure he recommended was basically an old folk remedy with bits and pieces of popular medical fads of the day thrown in. During his career Cayce gave thousands of medical readings. Today Cayce disciples insist that he was about 85 percent accurate and successful. Medical authorities hotly dispute this claim. But this is not a book about unconventional medicine; what we are really interested in is Cayce's career as a prophet. It grew directly out of his medical readings.

Once Cayce's career got going, he had someone write down what he said while he was in a trance. Thousands of these "readings" are now on file in the offices of the Association for Research and Enlightenment (ARE) in Virginia Beach, Virginia, an organization founded by Cayce admirers. His statements were rarely straightforward prescriptions, like "take two aspirin and call me in the morning." His prose was always tortured and his words rambling. Sometimes they rambled far afield. In some cases he would diagnose a patient's troubles as stemming from something that happened in a previous life. This implied reincarnation, a belief that was completely unacceptable to the fundamentalist Christianity that Cayce had grown up with and still professed. This conflict was never really resolved.

In addition to talking about people's past lives, he would sometimes ramble on and talk about the future. During Cayce's lifetime he was best known as a medical clairvoyant. Since his death in 1945, it is his prophetic utterances that have done the most to keep his reputation alive.

According to Cayce, many of those who sought his medical advice had past lives on the lost continent of Atlantis. Most scientists and historians insist that there never was a continent of Atlantis and that the legend began with the destruction of a small volcanic island off the coast of Greece that had erupted. But this is far too tame an explanation for many, and the search for the lost continent has been popular for a long time, particularly among those inclined toward the mystic and the occult.

In December 1943, Cayce predicted that Atlantis would rise again. He set no exact date for the event, and since his statements are always obscure, they are open to a wide range of interpretation. The key phrase is "in Atlantis in the period of the first upheavals and destruction that came to the land as must in the next generation come to other land."

It has been an article of faith among many believers in the lost continent that Atlantis would somehow rise again and that this would be the beginning of a series of worldwide cataclysms. Cayce followers first interpreted the sleeping prophet's words to mean that the destructive upheavals would take place within the generation following the time the prediction was made. A generation is usually counted as thirty-three years, therefore the destruction seems to have been predicted to take place before the end of 1976. It didn't happen. But as we shall see very shortly, other portions of the Cayce readings indicated a different, and somewhat later, date.

"The greater portion of Japan must go into the sea."

"The greater change, as we will find in America will be the North Atlantic Seaboard. Watch New York! . . . Portions of the now east coast of New York, or New York City itself, will in the main disappear."

Cayce didn't quite predict doomsday, but the magnitude of disasters he did predict sounds pretty close. One of the reasons that Cayce and his followers chose Virginia Beach as a headquarters was that they believed that it would be one of the relatively few safe places in the United States once the upheavals began.

In the mass of confusing and often contradictory predictions concerning the rising of Atlantis and the sinking of much of the rest of the world, Cayce gave some other dates: "Poseida will be among the first portions of Atlantis to rise again—expect it in '68 and '69—not so far away." This well-publicized Cayce prediction was one of the factors that set off a modest but very real end-of-the-world scare in 1968. (Another was the close approach of the asteroid called Icarus. For more information see Chapter 9.) The doomsday fears in 1968 were felt most deeply in California, a state that has more than its share of psychics and their followers. Californians also live with the constant threat of earthquakes and the overhanging threat that "the Big One" will truly devastate the region. Any well-publicized prediction, no matter how unreliable the source, is likely to inflame these fears. And so it was in 1968 and early 1969.

Subjects like Atlantis and reincarnation were not part of Cayce's fundamentalist background. But as his reputation as a medical clairvoyant grew, he attracted a following with occult and mystic interests. They introduced him to these concepts, which then increasingly began to appear in his "readings."

In the original Atlantis story told by Plato, Atlantis was an island continent in the Atlantic off the coast of Spain. Not only have scientists found no evidence for the existence of such a continent, most consider it a geological impossibility as well. Occultists seeking Atlantis have not limited their search to the middle of the Atlantic. They have "discovered" the island continent in a huge variety of unlikely places. Cayce indicated that Atlantis would begin to rise near the Bahamas, islands in the Atlantic off the southeastern coast of Florida. What is more, in the mid-1960s some of his followers insisted that they had found evidence of the sunken continent just where Cayce said it would be and that there were even indications that the underwater landmass was beginning to rise! Such tales got a surprising amount of publicity and helped to keep the doomsday pot boiling. In the end, it turned out that all of these stories were based on inaccurate or misinterpreted information, wild speculation, and just plain fraud. The Cayce followers never admitted they were wrong. They simply stopped talking about Atlantis.

Currently Atlantis is not popularly discussed as an omen or trigger for a world-ending series of catastrophes. But it is a belief that has been around for centuries and has proved to be remarkably tenacious. In one form or another it will surely be back.

The late Jeane Dixon never attained the status nor the following of an Edgar Cayce. For years her name appeared on a syndicated astrology column. She regularly made celebrity predictions for the supermarket tabloids and wrote a book on how to cast a horoscope for your dog. Dixon didn't claim to use astrology for her most celebrated predictions. She said she had visions, used a crystal ball, and employed some sort of clairvoyance when she touched a subject's fingertips. Dixon became just one of a large number of would-be modern prophets. But at one time she had the reputation of being much more.

Dixon, who was based in Washington, D.C., made a lot of political prognostications. The one that made her famous was this: In an article printed in *Parade* magazine

Jeane Dixon specialized in political predictions.

in 1956 she predicted that a Democrat would be elected to the presidency in 1960 and that he would either be assassinated or die in office, though not necessarily in his first term. Democratic candidate John F. Kennedy was elected in 1960, and he was assassinated.

The prediction, however, is a good deal less remarkable than it sounds. It is a curious fact that every president elected at twenty-year intervals, starting in 1840, had either been assassinated or had died in office, though not necessarily during the first term. The phenomenon even has a name, the "fatal twenty cycle," and has been well known in mystic and occult circles. Dixon simply did what many other prophets have done—she appropriated a popular belief and reported it as her own prediction. She did correctly predict that a Democrat would be elected, but her chances of being right were one in two—not very long odds. Besides, shortly before the 1960 election Dixon contradicted her earlier prediction by stating that Richard Nixon, then the Republican candidate, would win the election. She was wrong, though Nixon did win the presidency in a later try.

The "fatal twenty cycle" has now been shown up as nothing more than a statistical coincidence. Ronald Reagan, the oldest man ever elected president, thus a man more likely to die in office, was first elected in 1980. He finished out two terms, surviving both serious illness and an assassination attempt. Still there might be some talk of disaster striking the president who wins election in the year 2000.

Like other prophets, Jeane Dixon had a particular political and social point of view that colored her prophecies. Her politics were of the far right, and she was a fervent anti-Communist. She predicted great things for Richard Nixon and never predicted that he would be driven from office by scandal. She predicted that the Soviets would invade the Middle East, that they would put submarines off the coast of South America, and that by 1990 they would be in the final phase of "absorbing the Western Hemisphere by all means necessary including atomic war if needed." None of these things happened—quite the reverse: In 1990 it was the Soviets, and not the West, that tottered on the edge of collapse.

In addition to political predictions, many of which are quite apocalyptic, she had also made predictions based on End Times biblical prophecy. For example, she stated that the Antichrist was born in the Middle East on February 5, 1962. She did not, however, give us his name.

Jeane Dixon used the "fatal twenty cycle" as the basis for her most celebrated prophecy. Most tabloid prophets tend to reflect popular fears or beliefs in their prophecies. With a good deal of doomsday talk already in the air, these prophets inevitably predict some sort of apocalypse by the year 2000. It appears as if a group of psychically gifted individuals is independently predicting the same events. That makes any individual prediction sound more respectable because it seems to be backed up by lots of others. In reality what you have is a crowd vying for public attention, repeating what many people half believe already.

In baseball a manager who has a team that loses a lot of games gets fired. In prophecy someone like Jeane Dixon could make a long string of spectacularly wrong predictions and still find an audience willing to listen to her next batch of predictions. How do tabloid seers get away with it? First, most people don't deeply believe in such prophecies. They may read them for entertainment value or perhaps think of them as interesting or possible, but they will not change their lives on the strength of a prophecy. Second, the prophecies are often ambiguously worded, so that the prophets can insist that they were not really wrong even when they were. Third, they tell people what they want to hear or already believe. And finally, by pure chance, sometimes they are right. Without any special powers or crystal ball, you or I could easily predict that in the next year there will be a major earthquake, political assassination, or war somewhere. We would almost certainly be correct in at least one of these predictions. Fire enough shots, marksmen say, and you are bound to hit something. For some people one correct prediction will erase the memory of a thousand wrong ones.

Every year skeptics compile a list of prophecies made by tabloid prophets during the previous year. Most of them are so wildly wide of the mark that it is clear that they are nothing more than random guesses. But these exposures don't seem to affect the popularity of the prophets one bit. In one way or another they have been with us since prehistoric times, and they will still be with us long beyond the time that they have so frequently predicted for the end of the world.

PYRAMIDS AND SPACESHIPS

8

All manner of objects and events have been credited with prophetic powers. In this chapter we are going to look at two of the most curious, the Great Pyramid of Egypt and the modern phenomena known as flying saucers or UFOs.

Hundreds of pyramids from the days of the pharaohs can be found in Egypt. The best known, by far, are the three on the Plain of Giza, just outside modern Cairo. And of these one really stands out. It is called the Great Pyramid, and it is by any measure the largest and most magnificent of all the Egyptian pyramids. When the ancient Greeks made a list of what they called the seven wonders of the world, the Great Pyramid was one of them. It is the only one of these ancient wonders that survives to the present day. Though it has been repeatedly plundered, its gleaming limestone facing stripped, and the virtual city of temples and tombs that once surrounded it reduced to rubble, the Great Pyramid remains an impressive pile, the most familiar symbol of ancient Egypt, and an irresistible tourist attraction, as it has been for centuries.

There is, or should be, no particular mystery about why the Great Pyramid and all the other Egyptian pyramids were built. They were to be tombs for the god-kings of ancient Egypt. The Great Pyramid was built for the pharaoh called Khufu or Cheops, who reigned about 2900 B.C. There is some genuine mystery, or at least scholarly disagreement, about exactly how the Great Pyramid was built. But virtually all scholars agree that the "secret" to the construction of this gigantic edifice was the use of simple tools and techniques by an enormous number of well-organized human laborers over a very long period of time. Building this single tomb required as much work, treasure, and time from the Egyptians as constructing the entire interstate highway system did from the citizens of the United States.

But there are those who have looked at the Great Pyramid, or heard about it, and decided that it could not be *just* a tomb for a king and that it certainly could not have been conceived of and constructed by the technologically primitive Egyptians. So for a long time the Great Pyramid has been invested with a mystic significance that it really doesn't deserve.

The Great Pyramid has figured heavily in the symbolism of many mystic cults and secret societies, such as the Masons and the Rosicrucians. There is a good chance that right now you have a picture of it close at hand. Get a dollar bill and look at the back. On the left side there is the pyramid topped with the representation of an eye. It is part of the Great Seal of the United States.

While the Great Pyramid may have fascinated the founders of our nation, using the pyramid for prediction—pyramidology—didn't begin until 1859. A London publisher named John Taylor issued a book titled *The Great Pyramid: Why Was It Built? And Who Built It?* Even in 1859 the answers to those questions were well known. But Taylor was a Christian zealot and was irritated by the thought that the heathen, idol-worshiping Egyptians could have constructed such a monument. Taylor decided that the pyramid had to have been designed by one of the biblical patriarchs, perhaps Noah himself, acting under divine orders. "He who built the ark was, of all men, the most competent to direct the building of the Great Pyramid," wrote Taylor.

As proof Taylor cited the measurements of the pyramid, which he claimed displayed a far greater scientific knowledge than could possibly have been possessed by the ancient Egyptians. Taylor pointed out that if you divide the monument's height into twice the side of its base, you obtain a fairly close approximation of *pi* (the ratio of diameter to circumference of a circle). The value of pi was first established by a Greek mathematician more than two thousand years after the pyramid was built.

Taylor never visited Egypt, and his book might well have been completely forgotten had his strange obsession not infected another and far more important man, Charles Piazzi Smyth, the astronomer royal of Scotland. Smyth did visit Egypt and spent months crawling around the Great Pyramid laboriously making measurements. His conclusion was that the pyramid contained truths that not even Taylor had suspected. According to Smyth, the Great Pyramid "revealed a most surprisingly accurate knowledge of high astronomical and geographical physics . . . nearly 1,500 years earlier than the extremely infantine beginnings of such things among the ancient Greeks."

The numerical correlations described by Smyth and his disciples seem amazing at first glance. But are they really? One of Smyth's followers, after describing all the fives that can be found in measurements of the pyramid, says: "This intense *fiveness* could not have been accidental."

Science writer and mathematical gamester Martin Gardner constructed a well-known parody of such numerical techniques. He wrote:

> *Just for fun, if one looks up the facts about the Washington Monument in the* World Almanac *he will find considerable fiveness. Its height is 555 feet and 5 inches. The base is 55 feet square, and the windows are set at 500 feet from the base. If the base is multiplied by 60 (or five times the number of months in a year), it gives you 3,300 which is the exact weight of the capstone in pounds. Also the word 'Washington' has exactly ten letters (two times five). And if the weight of the capstone is multiplied by the base, the result is 181,500—a fairly close approximation of the speed of light in miles per second.*

The point of this exercise is, of course, to show that if you have enough numbers to play with, you can "prove" practically anything.

But such speculations on the Great Pyramid are of only secondary interest here. What is more important is that Smyth adopted and elaborated on the theories of his fellow countryman Robert Menzies. It was Menzies's idea that measurement of the internal passages of the pyramid provided a great outline of history—past, present, and future. The arrangements of the passages were sort of an allegory in stone.

According to the pyramidologists, history began with the creation of Adam in the year 4004 B.C. Humankind continued downward as symbolized by the Descending Passage, until the time of Christ. This was marked by the juncture of the Descending Passage with the Ascending Passage. Non-Christians continued in the Descending Passage to an underground chamber that represented Hell, while Christians went upward toward a larger passage called the Grand Gallery. The Grand Gallery leads to the King's Burial Chamber, which to the pyramidologist represented the glory of the Second Coming.

By measuring the Grand Gallery, Smyth calculated that the Second Coming would occur sometime between 1882 and 1911. This twenty-nine-year period, he believed, would be a time of great tribulation before the Second Coming. Smyth died in 1900, so he never did live to see that his prophetic chronology wasn't going to work out.

Smyth's work had a mighty appeal to some Christian fundamentalists who also disliked the "heathen" Egyptians and were glad to see that "science" was finally providing proof that the literal interpretation of the Bible was the correct one.

One of those attracted to pyramidology was Charles Taze Russell, the Pennsylvania clothing manufacturer who began the organization that later became Jehovah's Witnesses. As we have already seen, Russell was also influenced by the Millerites and the Adventist movement. Russell and

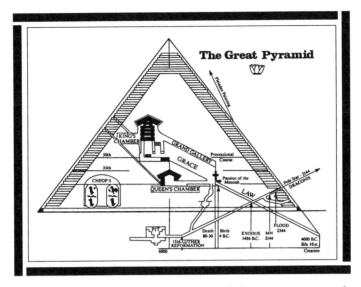

*Pyramidologists' interior diagram of the Great Pyramid,
showing the prophetic meaning of inside passages.*

others believed that the Great Pyramid showed that the
Second Coming would take place in 1914. That was the
year World War I broke out. But when the world failed to
end as predicted, some fell away from the sect. Russell's
successor, Judge J. F. Rutherford, abandoned pyra-midology
and declared that the Great Pyramid was really inspired by
Satan.

The pyramidologists and others of their kind have rarely
been discouraged by failure, for they could always recalculate and come up with new prophecies. In Smyth's day the
true measurements of the Great Pyramid were not known.
Lacking an exact standard of measurement, the
pyramidologists invented one, or rather they invented several, employing such units as the "pyramid inch." At one

time there was a movement in this country to revise our measuring system to conform to "sacred Pyramid standards" and to combat the "atheistic metrical system" that was a product of the French Revolution. Indeed, there is still to this day a great deal of resistance in the United States to adopting the metric system, which is in use throughout most of the rest of the world.

Ironically, the man who did the most to bring about the decline in pyramidology was originally one of Smyth's supporters. His name was William Flinders Petrie. At the age of thirteen, Petrie had first read Smyth's work, and he was determined to see for himself whether the theories were correct. Petrie became a professional surveyor, and at the age of twenty-six he set off for Egypt with boxes of measuring instruments. For years he measured and calculated with a single-minded passion. But unlike Smyth, Petrie was not blinded by preconceived notions.

One by one Smyth's miraculous correlations fell before Petrie's careful measurements. When Petrie finally published his monumental work on the pyramid, he remarked that he had never suspected that it would be he who "would reach the ugly little fact which killed the beautiful theory." Since the 1920s the popularity of pyramidology has been on the decline. But it has never disappeared. Later pyramidologists have found evidence, in the measurements of the chambers and passages, of predictions of the Great Depression, the rise of Adolf Hitler, the emergence of the state of Israel, and much more. They have also found in their calculations evidence of yet another date on which the world will end. John Cournos writes in *The Book of Prophecy*: "The pyramid does not vouchsafe us any prophecy beyond the year 2001."

The British mathematician and philosopher Bertrand Russell wrote of pyramidology:

I like also the men who study the Great Pyramid, with a view to deciphering its mystical lore. Many great books have been written on this subject, some of which have been presented to me by their authors. It is a singular fact that the Great Pyramid always predicts the history of the world accurately up to the date of the publication of the book in question, but after that date it becomes less reliable. Generally the author expects, very soon, wars in Egypt, followed by Armageddon and the coming of the Antichrist, but by this time so many have been recognized as Antichrist that the reader is reluctantly driven to skepticism.

From the Great Pyramid to outer space may seem like quite a leap, but it isn't really, at least not in the minds of some people. There are those who theorize that the Great Pyramid was not built by the Egyptians or by Noah, but by advanced beings from outer space.

Beginning in 1947, people reported seeing strange lights or objects in the sky. These were first dubbed "flying saucers" and later given the more dignified label Unidentified Flying Objects, or simply UFOs. It was assumed by many that these objects were not unidentified at all, that they were spaceships from other planets. Why had these spaceships suddenly begun hovering around earth? Not too many years earlier the first atomic bombs had been dropped on Japan, and even more powerful weapons were under development. The United States and the Soviet Union were locked in a tense struggle called the Cold War that threatened at any moment to erupt into a nuclear war and that might very well be the cataclysm that would bring the world to an end.

Among the many theories about the UFOs that were floated about, a popular one was that the space people had arrived to warn us of the dangers we had created and perhaps to save us from ourselves. Flying saucers became incorporated into the general atmosphere of mystic and prophetic lore. The head of one flying saucer group claimed that Jesus was about to return in a flying saucer. Others received "messages" from the space people warning of impending doom.

A lot of people toyed around with such notions, but a few took them very seriously and formed little UFO cults that anxiously or eagerly awaited the world's end. One such cult was formed in the Midwest in the 1950s and achieved a modest sort of immortality because it was infiltrated by psychologists from the University of Minnesota who were able to provide a very good inside look at how such groups think and operate.

This cult was led by a woman who claimed that messages she had received from the space people indicated that the city in which they were living was going to be destroyed by a flood from the Great Lakes. The flood would then spread across the continent to form an inland sea stretching from the Arctic Circle to the Gulf of Mexico. At the same time, according to the prophet, a cataclysm would submerge the West Coast from Seattle, Washington, to Chile in South America. This was a fairly standard prophecy of doom. In fact, the prophet of this cult, whom the

A well-known 1967 snapshot of a UFO taken by two Michigan youths. The boys estimated that the craft hovered over nearby Lake St. Clair for ten minutes.

psychologists called Mrs. Keech (a pseudonym), had been through a whole range of occult beliefs before she gained momentary fame with her prophecies from space.

What made this particular group unusual was that Mrs. Keech set a definite date, December 21, for the start of the cataclysm. The night before the city was to be flooded, Mrs. Keech said that she and her little band of associates would be picked up by a flying saucer and saved from the waters. They were to stand in the backyard of Mrs. Keech's house to await the arrival of the spaceship at exactly midnight of the twentieth.

The instructions from space were very specific. None of the group could have any metal on them. The reasons were not clear, but the order was taken seriously. The psychologist-observers noted:

All the believers complied painstakingly with this order. Arthur Bergen (another pseudonym provided by the University researchers), for example, carefully unwrapped the tinfoil from each stick of chewing gum in his pocket. Coins and keys were removed from pockets and watches from wrists. . . .

By 11:30 all was in readiness . . . when Arthur Bergen suddenly remembered that his shoes had metal toecaps, it was too late to cut them out. From the ensuing excitement emerged the suggestion that he should simply loosen the laces and step out of his shoes before entering the saucer. At about 11:35 one of the authors let it be known that he had not removed the zipper from his trousers. This produced a near-panic reaction. He was rushed into the bedroom where Dr. Armstrong (a pseudonym), his hands trembling and his eyes darting to the clock every few seconds, slashed out the zipper with a razor blade and wrenched its clasps free with wire cutters. By the time the operation was complete it was 11:50, too late to do more than sew up the rent with a few rough stitches. Midnight was almost at hand and everyone must be ready on the dot.

Midnight came and went and there was no flying saucer. Morning came and there was no great flood, except a flood of jeers from the skeptics. One might imagine that the normal human reaction would be to admit that you had been wrong, get angry at the person who had put you in such an embarrassing position, or simply try to sneak away and hide. This was not what Mrs. Keech and her followers did, and as the psychologists point out, true believers in prophecy rarely act that way. Their usual reaction is just the opposite of what one might expect. The true believers try harder than ever to convince others of the truth of their belief. That is exactly what the Millerites did when the world failed to end on one of the first dates that they had predicted.

Mrs. Keech and her followers, who had once been reluctant to talk to the press and public, now eagerly sought out every publicity outlet they could find. They were never exactly clear about why the flying saucer had not come and why the city had not been flooded. One idea was that their faith was being tested. Another was that the language of the prophecies had been misinterpreted and that the cataclysm would still take place. The believers were absolutely clear about one thing—the prophecy itself had not been wrong.

This group of believers was neither insane nor stupid; some might be considered a bit strange, but most were quite intelligent and highly educated people. What had happened to these people was that they had become deeply committed to a belief, so deeply committed that they could not imagine the possibility that the belief might be wrong. When events showed that without any doubt the belief was wrong, this created a great deal of psychological tension. The University of Minnesota psychologists said that one way of reducing this tension was: "If more and more people can be persuaded that the system of belief is correct, then clearly it must, after all, be correct. Consider the extreme case: If everyone in the whole world believed something, there would be no question at all as to the validity of the belief." According to the psychologists, that is why the believers tried harder than ever to surround themselves with more supporters after they were shown to be wrong. This reduces the psychological tension to the point where the believer can live with it.

The little band of believers who had gathered around Mrs. Keech broke up within a few weeks after the cataclysm failed to materialize. Despite their efforts they won no new converts. The psychologists concluded:

> *They were unskillful proselytizers. It is interesting to speculate, however, on what they might have made of their opportunities had they been more effective. . . . For about a week they were headline news throughout the nation. Their ideas were not without popular appeal, and they received hundreds of visitors, telephone calls, and letters from seriously interested citizens as well as offers of money (which they invariably refused).*

Events had conspired to offer them a truly magnificent opportunity to grow in numbers. Had they been more effective, [the failure of the spaceships to appear] might have portended the beginning and not the end.

Flying saucer groups are still around, though they rarely attract a large following, or much attention anymore. In 1997, however, one of these cults certainly got everyone's attention.

In March of that year police entered a large rented villa in an exclusive San Diego suburb and found the bodies of thirty-nine identically dressed individuals, twenty-one women and eighteen men aged twenty to seventy-two. There had been no violence. It was a mass suicide.

The thirty-nine were members of a UFO cult called Heaven's Gate. The group had been started more than two decades earlier by two Texans: a onetime music professor, Marshall Herff Applewhite, and a nurse, Bonnie Lu Trousdale Nettles. Calling themselves among other things "the Two" and "Bo and Peep," they led a nomadic existence preaching about flying saucers and higher planes of existence to small audiences in the West and Midwest. Though hundreds had probably fallen under their influence at one time or another, they were never able to hold a large following for long.

While the doctrine the two preached was fuzzy and ever-shifting, at its core was a belief that a spaceship would arrive to carry the group to another planet—and this would happen soon. It didn't, and at some point during the late 1980s Nettles died.

For Applewhite the arrival of the Hale-Bopp comet in 1997 was the signal. There was an erroneous report that the comet was being followed by a second object. Applewhite decided that this must be the long-awaited spaceship. But now cult members would not be transported physically—only spiritually. They would have to leave their "containers," or bodies, behind.

Before their final act most in the group made video-tapes in which they stated very clearly that what they were about to do was entirely voluntary, and that they were genuinely looking forward to leaving this plane of existence for the next. They looked and sounded happy. The tapes were chilling to watch.

Daniel Smith, a leader of the Unarian Society, one of the oldest and largest of the UFO groups, said that the members of Heaven's Gate had made a tragic mistake. They didn't have to kill themselves to meet the space people. And besides, they got the date wrong. The spaceship isn't scheduled to arrive until 2001!

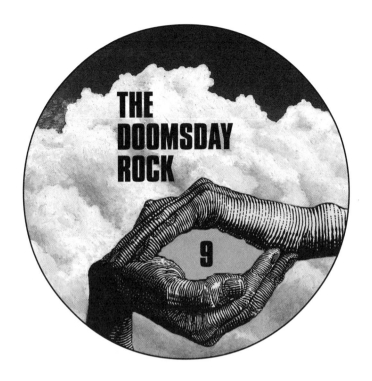

THE DOOMSDAY ROCK

9

What may turn out to be the scariest doomsday prediction has come not from any prophets or seers but from scientists.

In March 1998 scientists at the Smithsonian Astrophysical Observatory in Cambridge, Massachusetts, announced that a mile-wide asteroid named 1997 XF11 was going to pass in the vicinity of the earth on Thursday, October 26, 2028. Calculations were still preliminary, but the best first estimate was that it would be within 30,000 miles (48,300 kilometers) of the earth.

That sounds like a long distance, but this is space we are talking about. The moon is 240,000 miles (386,000 kilometers) away, so 30,000 miles is close. It might even be visible from earth as it flew by.

Dr. Brian Marsden, who made the announcement, stressed that there was still "some uncertainty to the computation. On the one hand, it is possible that 1997 XF11 will come scarcely closer than the moon. On the other hand, the object could come significantly closer than the moon."

Could the asteroid hit the earth?

"I would say that this thing probably won't hit us," Dr. Marsden said. That was not an entirely reassuring statement. The scientist figured that over the next few years we should have a better idea of how close this asteroid will come to earth. It takes about twenty-one months to circle the sun. It will be back again in the year 2000 and again in 2002. By that time, Dr. Marsden said, we should know how great the danger may be. "All we know right now is that the asteroid will come interestingly close in 2028—probably much closer than any asteroid recorded by astronomers in the past."

Within a day other scientists rushed out with more reassuring predictions. With new data they calculated that the asteroid would only come within 600,000 miles (965,000 kilometers) of earth, well beyond the orbit of the moon, and that the possibility of a collision with earth in 2028 was virtually zero.

Even Dr. Marsden, who had made the original announcement, backed off a bit from his first prediction. "From new data we have analyzed," he said, "I would agree that the probability of an impact seems smaller than it did, but it is not zero."

He continued, "We simply do not have sufficient knowledge of this object to be sure. Even if its present trajectory is capable of carrying it safely past earth, any small perturbation could put it on earth's track. The asteroid might be diverted toward the earth by gravitational inter-action with another asteroid, for example."

Other scientists agreed that calculating the exact orbit of an asteroid thirty years in the future is not really an exact science yet.

The story of the possible close encounter with an aster-oid made headlines all over the country, and in Hollywood the sound of cheering could be detected, for studios had two major asteroid disaster films scheduled to be released in the summer of 1998.

What with all the apocalyptic fears that are stirred up by the approach of the new millennium there is little doubt that an enormous amount of attention is going to be fo-cused on asteroid 1997 XF11 and any other large space rocks in the vicinity of our planet over the next few years.

Actually, fears about the doomsday possibilities of a col-lision between earth and a large asteroid have been grow-ing for some time, primarily because of what scientists have learned about the episode in the history of life on our planet known as The Great Death. It was a period of mass extinc-tion of species that took place 65 million years ago. The most famous victims were the dinosaurs.

We all know that the dinosaurs are extinct. For a long time it was assumed that they had died out because they had become too big, clumsy, and stupid to adapt to a chang-ing world. The word *dinosaur* became synonymous with anything that was oversized and unworkable. But the as-sumption never really made sense. The dinosaurs had been around for more than a hundred million years. During that period the earth had changed dramatically, and the dino-saurs had successfully adapted to all of those changes. They ruled the land. Yet at the end of the geologic period called the Cretaceous all the dinosaurs were gone. Gone too were a number of other species, from large amphibians to many species of tiny marine invertebrates.

Extinction is a natural process that has taken place throughout the history of life on earth. The vast majority of the species that have ever existed are now extinct. But it is usually a gradual and slow process. Throughout their long history many species of dinosaurs had evolved and become extinct. Before the end of the Cretaceous period, the heavily armed stegosaurs were long gone. The gigantic sauropods, such as *Brontosaurus*, had been greatly reduced in numbers. But there were enormous herds of duckbill dinosaurs and horned dinosaurs such as *Triceratops*. The smaller, swifter dinosaurs were more numerous than ever. The fossilized remains of these dinosaurs abound in the rocks of the late Cretaceous. Then the dinosaurs drop out of the fossil record, and scientists assume that they became extinct. Not entirely extinct perhaps. Many scientists believe that one type of dinosaur developed feathers and evolved into birds. All the rest disappeared.

The fossils can't tell us whether this apparent mass extinction took place overnight or over a period of a hundred or even a thousand years or more. But given the usual pace of extinction, the disappearance of the dinosaurs and so many of their contemporaries seems freakishly abrupt.

The first explanation that springs to mind is that there was some sort of worldwide catastrophe. Up until the middle of the nineteenth century most people in the West, even most scientists, believed that the earth was periodically swept by catastrophic events, such as the flood described in the Bible. Then a succession of geologists proved that most of the earth's features had been formed slowly over eons. They could find no evidence of regular catastrophes, and the belief faded. Scientists searched for other explanations for the death of the dinosaurs, such as changes in climate and vegetation. None of these explanations, however, proved very satisfactory, even to the people who had offered them. Catastrophic theories were still being advanced, but usually by crackpots. This alone made responsible scientists very wary of entertaining any catastrophic ideas.

By the late 1960s increased interest in the subject of dinosaurs in general inspired scientists to take a new look at the mystery of their extinction. Quite suddenly catastrophic theories were back. One theory that gained temporary popularity was that the earth had been bombarded with a dose of penetrating and deadly radiation, perhaps from an exploding supernova. The radiation didn't need to be intense enough to cause immediate death. Far lower doses can damage a creature's reproductive organs and render it sterile. At still lower doses radiation produces a higher number of stillbirths and mutations. Mutations are generally harmful and lower the survival potential of a species.

But no evidence of a nearby supernova or increased radiation bombardment from any source turned up. The popularity of the theory faded.

Another theory that emerged at that time, and did not go away, was that the earth had been struck by a huge meteorite or small asteroid. The impact would not only have killed large numbers of creatures at once but would have triggered vast climate changes that would have doomed the dinosaurs and many other species. A variety of evidence, not absolutely conclusive but very persuasive, has piled up to support this theory.

Once again the theory is not an entirely new one. All an astronomer has to do is take a look at the pitted surface of the moon to know that it has been struck repeatedly by meteorites large and small throughout history. Because the earth has an atmosphere, small meteorites burn up before they reach the surface. Larger meteorites do occasionally crash through the atmosphere and hit the surface of the earth. If they are large enough, they can leave an impact crater of substantial size. Since most of the earth's surface is covered with water, most meteorites would land in the water, where they might not leave an observable crater. The problem in recognizing any ancient meteorite craters on the land is that erosion and other geologic activity, such as mountain building, would tend to wear away or obscure the characteristic features of an impact crater. To confuse matters further, there are a variety of geophysical processes that can create features that look like impact craters but are not.

The largest generally recognized meteorite crater in the world is in the Arizona desert. It is called Barringer Crater, Arizona Crater, or most popularly and incorrectly Meteor Crater. (Strictly speaking, a meteor is the flash of light created by a meteorite as it burns up in the atmosphere.) Whatever you call it, this is everybody's idea of what an impact crater should look like. It is an almost perfect circle, 4/5 of a mile (1.2 kilometers) across, with a circumference of nearly 3 miles (5 kilometers). You could drop the Washington Monument in the middle of the crater and only 6 feet (2 meters) of it would stick up over the rim. What is more, the crater was once deeper, but the action of weather has filled it in somewhat. The original impact pulverized and blew out some 300 million tons of rock.

The Barringer Crater is named after a mining engineer named Daniel Barringer, who started mining operations there in 1903. The buildings on the right side of the crater are a visitors' center and housing for scientists.

No one is really sure how large the meteorite had to have been, or what sort of havoc resulted. Estimates of size range between 80 and 500 feet (24 and 150 meters) in diameter. The impact would doubtless have been catastrophic to life for perhaps 100 miles (160 kilometers) in each direction, and the dust cloud thrown off would probably have traveled around the world. But the impact that created the Barringer Crater took place within the last 50,000 years—far too recently to have had anything to do with the death of the dinosaurs. Besides, the crater is much too small to have resulted in the kind of worldwide cataclysm envisioned by those who think a collision with an asteroid caused the mass extinctions of the Cretaceous period.

There are, however, other scars on the earth's surface that may have been caused by the impact of far later meteorites or asteroids. Currently the most popular site for the impact of the object that ended the reign of the dinosaurs is the coast of the Yucatán Peninsula in Mexico. The object that struck there is estimated to have been about 6 miles (10 kilometers) in diameter and released some five billion times more destructive energy than the bomb that leveled Hiroshima.

Powerful as it would have been, the impact itself would not have caused the worldwide extinctions. The real killer would be the aftereffects. The collision would have thrown up dust clouds thick enough to block most of the sunlight coming to earth for three or four years. "Turning off the light" in this way would not only lower the world's temperature it would also profoundly affect the growth of plants. Without a huge supply of plants to feed their massive bodies, the large plant-eating dinosaurs would soon die. The giant carnivores would follow them into extinction. Speculation about a dust cloud also fueled the discussion of the "nuclear winter" theory that got a great deal of attention in the early 1980s. In this theory the smoke and dust from even a relatively small nuclear war would create a cloud that would drastically alter the world's climate.

It must be pointed out that many paleontologists, the scientists who know the most about dinosaurs, don't think a single catastrophe caused their extinction. They note that the number of dinosaur species had been in decline for some time before all the species disappeared at the end of the Cretaceous. The mass death, they say, was not nearly as rapid or dramatic as has been popularly portrayed. As evidence for a cataclysmic collision 65 million years ago piles up, however, they do admit that it may have at least contributed to the extinction of the dinosaurs.

The greatest collision of a large astronomical object with earth to take place in historic times was on June 30, 1908. The site of the impact was in a very remote section of Siberia. What hit the earth was probably a fragment of a comet, essentially a piece of ice with small pieces of rock embedded in it, or what is called a stony meteorite, a conglomerate of small stones rather than one large solid object, for there was no large crater at the point of impact. The region was barely populated so there are no reliable eyewitness accounts of the event. People 50 miles (80 kilometers) away saw the flames and were knocked over by the shock waves. There was a gigantic explosion that registered on seismographs, the instruments used for measuring earthquakes, throughout the world. The dust and smoke cloud from the collision created brilliant sunsets throughout the Northern Hemisphere for years. The impact area was so remote that outside observers didn't visit the scene for over a decade. But even that many years after the event the signs of devastation were overwhelming. Trees in an area of 25 miles (40 kilometers) around the center of the impact were uprooted and charred. And this was all caused by a relatively small object.

Wandering throughout our solar system are quite a number of asteroids that can come pretty close to earth. Astronomers have identified 108 "potentially hazardous objects," or PHOs, that are possible threats to the earth over the next few centuries. They estimate that ten times that number remain undetected. The fact is that nobody really knows.

In 1968 the close approach of an asteroid called Icarus set off a small but very definite end-of-the-world scare. There had already been rumors that a series of worldwide cataclysms was going to begin in 1968. When news got around that Icarus was heading toward the earth and would make its closest approach on June 15, 1968, it became a link in the public's mind with the other end-of-the-world rumors. In California some people headed for the mountains of Colorado, saying that they wanted to be on safe ground before the asteroid hit the sea and created tidal waves that would cause California to sink into the ocean. Actually there is no way of calculating just where an asteroid might strike earth. But since the planet is mostly ocean, the ocean is a pretty good bet.

Those who thought that they would awaken on the morning of June 15 and see the great mass of Icarus rushing through the sky were disappointed—and probably relieved. Unlike comets that vaporize and glow brilliantly, asteroids do not glow and are very hard to spot. Icarus could be traced only with difficulty by the most sophisticated and sensitive radar available. It was still millions of miles from earth. In astronomical terms that is close, but it does not represent a threat.

Astronomers were amused, puzzled, or angered by all the excitement. They knew Icarus wasn't going to hit the earth. It had been close to earth before, closer in fact. And in previous years there had been much closer approaches by large asteroids. In 1937 an asteroid called Hermes skimmed within a mere 485,000 miles (780,000 kilometers) of earth on October 30. That was still twice as far away as the moon, but it was the closest known approach of an asteroid to earth.

In March 1998, when all the excitement over asteroid 1997 XF11 broke out, some Russian scientists reported that Icarus is again bearing down on the earth. In fact, Icarus probably won't come within 5 million miles (8 million kilometers) of earth this time.

Writing in *The New York Times*, author William E. Burrows said: "One suspects these scientists have a screenplay in the works—the Russian equivalent, perhaps, of Steven Spielberg's forthcoming *Deep Impact*." He might have added Disney's *Armageddon*, the other big budget asteroid disaster film of 1998.

If an asteroid the size of Icarus, which is some 7 miles (11 kilometers) in diameter and weighs several hundred tons, struck the earth, that would truly be a doomsday scenario. A collision with 1997 XF11, only about a mile in diameter, would create gigantic tidal waves, and an eruption of dust that could cause global cooling and long term disruption of agriculture. But Dr. Marsden said such an asteroid impact would not necessarily be severe enough to wipe out the human race. Still, it would not be a cheery prospect.

Astronomers really know a good deal less about the comings and goings of these asteroids than you might suspect. In space an object a mile or two in diameter and reflecting only a faint light is very hard to find. By the time the asteroids come close enough to be seen, they are going so fast across the sky that it requires luck as well as skill to keep track of them. Several observatories as well as NASA and the Air Force have programs for tracking near-earth asteroids, but none of these programs is very large and scientists complain that to date the effort is underfunded and disorganized.

Since no one is really sure how many potentially dangerous objects are out there, estimates of the chances of earth being struck by an asteroid—though not necessarily anything as large as the doomsday rock—vary wildly.

One authority, Dr. Tom Gehrels of the Lunar and Planetary Laboratory at the University of Arizona, said, "We have calculated on the basis of what we know of the earth's impact history that during a human life span of 66 years, there is a 1 in 5,000 chance of a major impact." He added, "That's a pretty big chance when you think about it."

In 1972 a fairly large meteorite—about the length of a football field—zipped through the upper atmosphere over the northern United States and Canada, blazing across the sky in a daylight fireball witnessed by thousands of people before it reentered space. This object was nowhere near the doomsday rock category, though if it had struck the earth it certainly would have been noticed. Luckily it missed.

If something disastrously large were found to be heading directly toward earth could it be stopped? Some scientists have suggested that given enough warning the object would be diverted or deflected by a rocket containing nuclear explosives. The aim would not be to blow the thing up. Even if that could be accomplished it would produce a myriad of smaller but still dangerous rocks that might rain down on earth. A much better and safer plan would be to use rocket-borne explosives to deflect the object from its collision course with our planet.

During the March 1998 excitement some news reports made it sound as if this would be an easy solution. In the opinion of Dr. Bruce Murray of the California Institute of Technology, "Big bombs are not practical. For one thing, delivering a bomb to a distant asteroid is no easy job. Right now we can't even seem to shoot down Iraqi Scud missiles. But we'll have to find a solution to the asteroid problem some day, and that day may be approaching."

At the present time there simply isn't any plan.

Still, virtually all of the experts agree that the chances of you, or your children, or your children's children or their children, etc., going the way of the dinosaurs are very slim indeed. But we also know that there is absolutely nothing more alarming than a group of experts sitting around saying that there is nothing to be alarmed about. We have all seen too many movies to believe that!

So it takes no prophetic powers to predict that no matter what we are told, as the millennium approaches we are going to become more and more worried about the dooms-day rock.

SIGNS IN
THE SKY AND
THE EARTH

10

According to the Bible, the end of the world will come
suddenly and without warning. But it is also assumed that
the coming end will be heralded by a whole variety of signs,
some political and some natural.

Historically one of the most powerful signs of approaching doomsday, or at least of some cataclysm, was the appearance of a comet in the sky. Asteroids are not mentioned
in the Bible. We have already seen how the appearance of a
comet in early 1843 helped to support the doomsday beliefs of the Millerites.

It is not surprising that in the past comets were regarded
as having an awesome and terrible significance. There have
been no bright comets this century, but a
really bright comet can be a truly spectacular celestial event.

It looks like a huge fireball in the sky with a blazing tail behind it. A comet just looks dangerous. A comet can be the brightest object in the night sky, outshining even the moon. Some comets have been so bright that they could be seen in the daytime.

The comet has not only been feared as an omen, but as an actual physical menace to the earth as well. It might smash into our planet and cause unimaginable damage. In ancient times, however, when people assumed that the earth was the largest object in the universe, people were less frightened of comets. Comets were probably regarded as just another luminous object in the night sky.

The Greek philosopher Aristotle believed that all astronomical objects—the sun, moon, planets, and stars—were regular and orderly. Comets were disorderly intruders. Therefore, Aristotle reasoned, comets could not be astronomical objects but were rather some sort of disturbance in the earth's atmosphere, caused by burning vapors from the ground. The implication was that comets were no danger to the earth, though Aristotle did note: "When there are many comets . . . the years are clear, dry, and windy." The winds, in Aristotle's opinion, were a by-product of the burning vapors.

The word *comet*, by the way, has a rather benign origin considering the awe in which these objects came to be held. It comes from the Greek word *kometes*, which means "long-haired." The comet was often described as a "long-haired star," the picture being the "star" or head of the comet with the long hair or tail trailing behind it.

Aristotle's rather mild view of comets was not shared by the majority of the people of his time. Astrology had gotten a firm hold on the minds of most people, including

Aristotle's own people. Attempting to divine the future by interpreting various natural events as signs, portents, or omens of things to come was an almost universal obsession among the Greeks.

To the astrologically minded the heavens were not so much a place of stars and planets as a book in which the gods or the fates had written out all of the future events in sign language. Everything that happened in the sky had to have some significance for earthly events. The only problem was figuring out the rules for interpreting the signs.

In theory, astrology is an orderly practice, and comets didn't seem to fit into an orderly scheme. A comet was a disruption in the normal order of things. So it's easy to see how the appearance of a large comet came to be regarded with such awesome significance in the ancient world. A disruption in the heavens meant disruption on the earth.

Though people believed that the appearance of a comet meant that something big was about to happen, they did not always agree on what the big event would be. Usually the comet was interpreted as foretelling something that the interpreter greatly wished or feared.

In the year A.D. 69 a comet was visible over the city of Jerusalem. Jewish rebels, driven in part by a belief and hope that the Messiah was about to come, were fighting a desperate battle against the Romans, who were trying to retake the city. Jewish prophets urged the people to climb to the roof of the Temple where they would see the miraculous sign of their coming deliverance that God had provided for them. They were wrong. The city was taken by the Romans the following year, and the Temple, holiest of Jewish holy places, was burned.

The seventeenth century combined great technical progress with crude superstition. This engraving depicts celestial signs that indicate a bad harvest is forthcoming.

Some Romans, on the other hand, interpreted the very same comet as an omen of doom for the emperor Vitellius. As it turned out, these Romans were quite right. Vitellius was one of Rome's least successful emperors. He ruled for less than a year and was murdered by the Roman mob.

The Jewish general Josephus, who switched to the Roman side after he was captured, interpreted the comet as a sign of the triumph of the Roman general Vespasian. Vespasian had crushed the Jewish revolt and replaced the unfortunate Vitellius as emperor. Of course Josephus made his "prediction" only after Vespasian, who became his friend and patron, was firmly in power.

As you can see, comets could mean all sorts of things. In the play *Julius Caesar* Shakespeare wrote:

When beggars die there are no comets seen;
The heavens themselves blaze for the death
of princes.

Throughout the Middle Ages comets were generally considered signs of God's wrath rather than his favor. For medieval Christians gloomy, even apocalyptic omens were much in fashion. Here is a typical quote from a listing of comets: "Anno 1531, 1532 and 1533 comets were seen and at that time Satan hatched heretics."

By the middle of the sixteenth century, science had begun to learn something about what comets really were. The Danish astronomer Tycho Brahe was able to calculate that most comets were a long way from the earth. Aristotle's old idea of comets being some sort of atmospheric disturbance was finally laid to rest.

In 1705, British astronomer Edmund Halley suggested that comets orbited the sun and that the same comets had been seen many times in history. Comets that had appeared in 1456, 1531, 1607, and 1682 were in reality one comet whose orbit brought it near the earth approximately every seventy-six years. He predicted that the comet would appear again in 1758 or 1759. He was right, and that comet now bears his name, Halley's comet.

Once it was established that comets were a regular feature of the solar system, not some sort of sudden and miraculous appearance, their reputation as omens was greatly diminished. But increased knowledge of comets raised a new fear. If they were a long way from the earth, then they must be huge, and what would happen if one of them swerved off course and struck the earth?

It was also determined that the glowing "tail" of a comet is created when frozen gases, which make up the bulk of

A sketch based on a medieval tapestry shows Halley's comet frightening the populace in 1066.

the comet, begin to vaporize as it nears the sun. Would the earth's atmosphere be poisoned by passing through the tail of a comet?

Both of these fears were triggered by the well-publicized 1910 appearance of Halley's comet. Astronomers pointed out that the head of the comet, the only solid part, wouldn't come within millions of miles of earth. There was no danger of a collision. Still, there was the fear that the comet's tail contained poisonous gases. One enterprising Englishman took to selling comet pills—a harmless mixture of aspirin and sugar—to protect people from the effects of the poisonous gases. The earth did, in fact, pass through the tail of Halley's comet in 1910, without any noticeable ill effects.

Despite all the excitement and fears about the arrival

of the famous comet, the 1910 appearance was no big deal for the general public. Most people couldn't see it at all, and those who could observed only a tiny, wispy streak in the sky. Halley's comet came back again in 1986. Once again there was a buildup of excitement, though by this time most people had become sophisticated enough about comets not to fall prey to apocalyptic fears. In 1986 the comet was even less impressive than it had been in 1910. In truth, Halley's comet is dying. Each time it makes a pass around the sun, more of it vaporizes, and one day it will disappear altogether.

We know that the danger of a comet actually striking the earth is a real possibility—though a remote one. But even today the comet retains some of its ancient power as a portent rather than an agent of doom. For much of the twentieth century there had been no bright comets, comets that could be seen easily with the naked eye. Then in 1997 the Hale-Bopp comet appeared. It didn't exactly light up the night sky, but it was far and away the brightest comet in well over a generation. No one alive had ever seen anything like it. The comet could easily be identified without the aid of a telescope. Hale-Bopp began to figure in all sorts of apocalyptic predictions, and its appearance inspired a small flying-saucer cult to commit mass suicide.

Historically, people who are addicted to cataclysmic theories are frequently addicted to comets as well. Back in 1696 the Reverend William Whiston of England advanced some theories about how the close approach of certain comets throughout history had profound effects on the earth. A comet, he said, had caused the biblical flood. Reverend Whiston was a respected mathematician, and his book *The*

An artist shows reactions to Halley's comet in 1910.

Cause of the Deluge Demonstrated, published in 1711, was extremely influential. Whiston had formed his theories before Halley's discovery. However, his ideas about comets and catastrophes were scientifically and historically unsound, even in his own day. He seems to have been more influenced by the comet's evil reputation than anything he had been able to calculate about them.

One of the great crank scholars of history was the nineteenth-century American Ignatius Donnelly. Donnelly was a successful, if unorthodox, politician who had served eight years in the House of Representatives and had run for vice president twice on the Populist Party ticket. But he is best known for his bizarre theories. His book about the "lost continent" of Atlantis is still sold today. He also proposed that the close approach of comets had triggered a series of worldwide catastrophes.

In more recent times a psychiatrist named Immanuel Velikovsky put forward a series of catastrophic theories that created a genuine popular controversy in the 1950s. The close approach of comets also figured heavily in his speculations. His books were best-sellers for years. Today Velikovsky is pretty much a forgotten historical figure, but a small band of disciples remains, and every once in a while they pop up to proclaim that "Velikovsky was right after all."

Earthquakes are another natural phenomenon that has been invested with apocalyptic significance. The Bible mentions "great earthquakes" as one of the signs foretelling the end of the world: "And I beheld when he had opened the sixth seal, and lo, there was a great earthquake; and the sun became black as sackcloth of hair, and the moon became as blood" (Revelation 6:12).

While eclipses and comets have also been looked upon

as signs of the coming end, they do no damage, and scientifically they have been well explained and can be predicted. Earthquakes, on the other hand, can be enormously destructive, and earthquake prediction remains an inexact science to say the least. Any "great earthquake" or apparent increase in earthquake activity is pointed to as a sign of the coming end by those who already believe the end is near.

There is, however, a problem in deciding what a "great earthquake" is. Is it an extremely powerful quake, or is it a quake in which there are many deaths and widespread destruction? The two may not necessarily be the same. In 1988 an earthquake in Soviet Armenia killed more than 25,000 people. In 1991 an earthquake in nearby Soviet Georgia killed several hundred people. But on the standard measurement of earthquake power, the Richter scale, the 1991 quake was much stronger. The main effects of the 1988 quake were felt in a more densely populated area, resulting in much higher fatalities.

The strongest quake ever recorded was centered in Chile in 1960. Some 10,000 perished, a terrifying tragedy, but the death toll was still far lower than that of the relatively mild Armenian quake. The most deadly of all earthquakes was the one that struck Shensi Province in central China in 1556—an estimated 830,000 people died. It was a powerful quake, but there were no instruments to accurately measure its power. The earthquake in China did not set off a rash of end-of-the-world predictions, because the Chinese were not influenced by Revelation 6:12. Those who were probably never even heard of the event that took place on the other side of the world. The Lisbon earthquake of 1755 did spark end-of-the-world predictions. An estimated 60,000 were killed, nowhere near the number that had died in China, but it was a catastrophe that took place in Christian Europe.

In the United States the focus of earthquake fears is the state of California. In fact, the most powerful earthquake ever recorded in the United States was the one that struck Alaska on Good Friday, 1964. Casualties were relatively light, but the quake displaced the earth's surface over an area of 100,000 square miles (259,000 square kilometers).

"The Great American Earthquake," the one that everyone thinks about, is the quake that devastated San Francisco in 1906. Although it was powerful, it was nowhere near as powerful as Alaska's Good Friday earthquake. Those Californians who like to minimize the earthquake dangers of the state insist that most of the deaths and destruction in 1906 were caused by the fires that followed the quake, not by the quake itself. Of course the fires were caused by the quake. At the time there were many who insisted that San Francisco, which had a reputation for immorality, had been destroyed for that reason, but there seems to have been no general end-of-the-world scare.

The earthquake scare of 1968–69 has already been mentioned. Although there had been lots of predictions of a major earthquake during that period, all the prophets missed the major quake that hit the San Fernando Valley in February 1971. They also missed the only earthquake covered live on prime-time nationwide television. It was the earthquake that shook the Oakland, California, area in 1989, just as a World Series game was beginning in Oakland. Although both the 1971 and 1989 earthquakes caused many deaths and lots of destruction, the toll was relatively light considering that they occurred in heavily populated areas. California may lead the world in constructing earthquake-resistant structures. California structures are very far from being earthquake-proof—there may be no such thing. But just compare the light death toll in heavily populated California to the enormous number of casualties in Soviet Armenia, and the advantages of modern engineering become obvious.

A self-appointed earthquake expert predicted that the American Midwest would experience a major quake in the fall of 1990 along what is called the New Madrid Fault. The prediction got a lot of media attention, but it was mostly lighthearted. People were more amused than frightened. There have been earthquakes in the Midwest, even powerful ones, and there could be another, but they don't occur very often. You can spend your entire life in the Midwest without ever experiencing even a minor earthquake. California is shaken regularly by minor earthquakes, and though some people insist that they "get used to them," the underlying fear remains.

What Californians fear is "the Big One." Earthquakes occur along cracks in the earth's surface called fault lines. The most notorious in California is the San Andreas Fault, an ominous-looking 600-mile (966 kilometer) crack that runs from Mendocino to the Gulf of California. Stress builds up along a fault, and when a readjustment of the two sides of the fault takes place, it can be rapid and violent. It is an earthquake.

There had been a major earthquake along the San Andreas Fault in 1857. The next one was the San Francisco earthquake of 1906, an interval of forty-nine years. Although there have been plenty of earthquakes in California, there has been no major release of tension along the San Andreas for nearly ninety years. One day it's going to

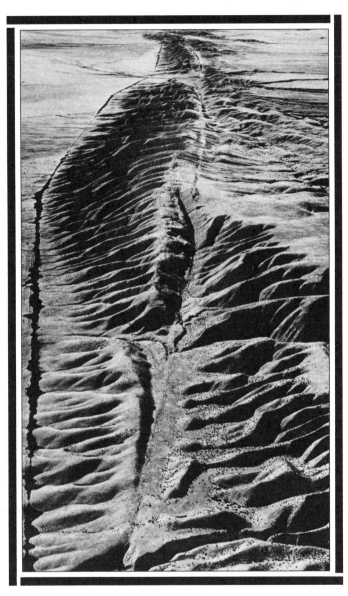

*An aerial view of
California's San Andreas fault.*

happen, and that will be "the Big One." No one can predict how destructive it will be. There are too many unknowns. Nor can anyone predict exactly when the earthquake will occur. It could be tomorrow or years from now. But virtually all scientists agree that there will be a major earthquake in California within this generation.

The almost certain knowledge that there will be a major California earthquake, coupled with the general doomsday predictions and fears that will be with us until at least the end of this millennium, will doubtless make Californians more nervous than ever. Any tremor, even any well-publicized prediction, no matter how ill informed, could set off a scare that would dwarf that of 1968–69. And if "the Big One" does occur between now and the year 2000, it will be held up as a sure sign that the end is near. But there have been "Big Ones" before, lots of them, and for better or worse, California is still here.

THE FOUR HORSEMEN

11

Perhaps the most striking and memorable image in the Book of Revelation is that of the four horsemen. The prophet sees a book with seven seals being opened, hears the sound of thunder, and four riders appear. They are often referred to as the four horsemen of the apocalypse.

The meaning of the first horseman, seated upon a white horse, is unclear. Some think the horseman is a symbol of Christ returning. Others disagree. But there is little disagreement about the grim meaning of the other three horsemen.

The rider on the red horse is war, the rider on the black horse famine, and the rider on the pale horse death, probably in the form of plague or pestilence. Thus three powerful symbols of the coming end of the world are great wars, great famines, and great epidemics.

In biblical times and indeed in the modern world the three are often interconnected. Wars bring about famines and epidemics. In the spring of 1991 the evening TV news was filled with pictures of starving refugees fleeing from the results of the war in the Persian Gulf. War, starvation, and disease, no matter how terrible, were not to actually bring about the end of the world. That would happen when the sky opened up and God purged the world with fire. The earthly disorders were merely signs of the coming end.

In the modern world, war, famine, and pestilence have taken on terrible new meanings. War has become progressively more horrible since biblical times. Not that humans are any crueler today than they were two thousand years ago. It's just that we have more efficient weapons. The most bloodthirsty and depraved Roman soldier could not in a lifetime of battle kill and maim as many people as a normally kind and humane pilot can on a single bombing run.

Our whole concept of war changed abruptly on August 6, 1945, when a U.S. bomber dropped an atomic bomb on the Japanese city of Hiroshima. The city was destroyed, and thousands of people were killed instantly in the blast. Many more died later from radiation burns and other injuries. A second and even more powerful atomic bomb was dropped three days later over the city of Nagasaki.

Thus in a flash of blinding light and searing heat did the atomic age open. It was a scene to rival the visions of the most apocalyptic of biblical prophets. The explosion of an atomic bomb created a huge mushroom-shaped cloud, and in a sense we have lived in the shadow of that mushroom-shaped cloud ever since.

The bombing of Hiroshima and Nagasaki may have helped to hasten the end of World War II. But immediately after the war, both the United States and the Soviet

And I saw and behold a white Horse, and he that sate
on him had a bowe, and there went out another horse y'
was red and there was given to him that sate theiron a
great sword v.I &4. And I beheld & lo a black horse. v.5.

The four horsemen of the apocalypse.

Union began building up their stockpiles of atomic bombs and, later, of the even more powerful hydrogen bombs. And both nations began to develop the means to deliver the bombs quickly and effectively. Soon other nations—Britain, France, and China—got their own nuclear weapons. It wasn't long before there were enough nuclear weapons to kill every man, woman, and child on earth several times over.

In the half a century that followed the end of World War II, there have been many crises, and on several occasions the world seemed on the brink of nuclear war. But it never happened. During this period there have been numerous smaller wars. *Small* here is a relative term, for some of these wars, such as the war in Vietnam and the war between Iran and Iraq, have killed millions. None, however, was a worldwide nuclear conflict.

In the early 1990s, European communism collapsed and the Soviet Union dissolved. The decades-long Cold War between the two great nuclear superpowers was over. The nuclear-tipped long-range missiles that each side had aimed at major cities of the other were turned away. Of course the weapons did not disappear. The missiles can be easily retargeted. So the threat of mutual nuclear annihilation remains. But even the most confirmed pessimist will admit that the threat is not nearly as great as it was just a few years ago.

The major problem now is that nuclear technology is no longer in the hands of just a few major powers. A growing number of smaller nations possess nuclear weapons, or are trying very hard to build them. It is not difficult to imagine how a nuclear war could be started by a relatively small nation under the control of a powerful and ruthless ruler.

What would the results of a nuclear war be? In theory such a war could destroy all life on earth. Even a relatively limited nuclear war might bring about so much environmental damage that while human life on earth might not become impossible, it would be very difficult and perhaps not worthwhile. Some scientists insist that such a scenario

A fireball from a nuclear explosion rises above the Nevada desert as part of a 1957 testing program.

is "alarmist" and that we could survive a nuclear war. Who's right? No one really knows, and no sane person really wants to find out. Even if the "optimists" are right, nuclear war on any scale wouldn't be pleasant.

War, the rider on the red horse, is now more than ever a symbol of the apocalypse.

Famine, the rider on the black horse, has also taken on

a ghastly new meaning in the modern world. Those of us who live in the industrialized world usually have more of a problem with eating too much rather than not finding enough to eat. But for people in many parts of the world, famine—total starvation, not just hunger—is a recurring nightmare.

In biblical times famines occurred regularly. A bad harvest might bring about mass starvation in many places where there was little or no reserve food. Over the centuries as civilization advanced, it seemed as though the problem of famine might finally be overcome.

In 1798 a pessimistic English curate named Thomas Malthus wrote a highly influential work called *An Essay on the Principle of Population.* "The power of population is infinitely greater than the power in the earth to produce substance for man," Malthus wrote.

"Population when unchecked, increases in a geometrical ratio. Substance increases only in an arithmetical ratio. A slight acquaintance with numbers will show the immensity of the first power in comparison with the second."

Malthus believed that starvation would provide the ultimate check on the growth of the human population, just as it does on the population of so many animal species: "By that law of nature which makes food necessary to the life of a man, the effects of these two unequal powers must be kept equal.

"This implies a strong and constantly operating check on population from the difficulty of substance."

For a while, Malthus's ideas were very widely believed. As agricultural technology advanced more rapidly than Malthus or anyone of his time could have foreseen, it looked as though he might be proved wrong. Much more food was being produced on less land by fewer workers. And modern transportation made it possible to get food to areas of temporary shortage before real starvation set in. A vastly increased population could and has been fed.

But in the long run Malthus's gloomy forebodings may turn out to be correct. Population is still outrunning food supply. In many nations the benefits of agricultural improvements have been wiped out by population growth.

As you read this sentence, five people will have died of starvation. Most of them will be children.

Mass famines are still very much a part of the modern world. As these words are being written, hundreds of thousands in Bangladesh face starvation as the result of disastrous floods. In Ethiopia and the Sudan, masses of refugees from seemingly endless civil wars are dying of hunger. For all our scientific and technical advances famine, the rider on the black horse, is still very much with us.

The rider on the pale horse, death in the form of plague or other epidemic disease, has also taken on a new meaning in today's world. There had, of course, been "plagues"— what we now call epidemics—since the dawn of history.

Perhaps the worst epidemic ever to hit the Western world was the Black Death (probably an epidemic of bubonic, or black, plague) that raged through Europe in the Middle Ages. The Black Death killed an estimated one fourth to one third of the population of Europe.

During the plague years there were numerous end-of-the-world panics. People didn't understand the reasons for the plague. The Black Death was thought to be divine punishment for wickedness. In plague-torn Europe, Judgment Day itself seemed very close at hand.

*Despite the advances of modern technology, famine
is still very much a part of the modern world.
Children are particularly affected.*

Slowly advances in medicine began to push back the specter of great epidemics. Once people learned what diseases were and how they were spread, effective steps could be taken to prevent them. It's not that deadly epidemics became a thing of the past or were limited only to the poor and backward nations. In 1918 an influenza epidemic killed half a million people in the United States and 20 million throughout the world. But even a catastrophe of this magnitude failed to set off end-of-the-world fears. Influenza was a known disease, and there were ways of successfully treating it.

The fourth horseman, it seemed, was under control. And then came AIDS. The AIDS virus destroys the human immune system and renders the body defenseless against a host of deadly diseases. It first came to notice in the United States about 1980. The vast majority of the victims were homosexual men.

For a while AIDS was ignored by the general population. Only when the news broke that people outside the gay community had contracted AIDS too did the seriousness of the epidemic hit home. The initial reaction was often fear. There were several reasons for this fear. AIDS was a new disease, and at first there was a lot that was unknown, or at least uncertain, about it. Once the disease developed, it was invariably fatal—there was no treatment and no cure.

Then there was the fact that the disease was spreading among homosexuals, a group that many condemned as immoral. It had been a long time since disease had been regarded as a punishment from God. To some, AIDS looked like exactly that.

During the mid-1980s, AIDS became a regular part of the presentations of apocalyptic preachers. Here surely was the rider on the pale horse. It was a new worldwide plague, a punishment from God for sin, and a clear sign that the world was in its last days.

Gradually the panic subsided as more became known about AIDS. Scientists established, beyond any doubt, how the AIDS virus spread. Although it couldn't be cured, AIDS could be avoided. Some reasonably effective treatments for the disease have been developed. AIDS is a terrible disease, but it is very definitely a disease, much like other terrible diseases. It is not a supergerm and certainly not a divine punishment for anything. Modern physicians do not view AIDS as medieval physicians viewed the Black Death. Someday, perhaps someday soon, there will be a vaccine to prevent the disease and possibly even a cure for it.

While mention of AIDS is still often cited as a sign of an approaching doomsday, it is no longer the fearful symbol that it was just a few years ago.

TOWARD THE YEAR 2000

12

There is no special religious significance attached to the year 2000. The Bible says nothing about the year 2000. Neither does any other document from ancient times.

The reason is quite simple: There was no concept of the year 2000 in ancient times.

The modern calendar really began in what we now call the sixth century when a monk named Dionysus Exiguus (translated that means Denis the Short, but it sounds better in Latin) was asked by the pope to make some calculations about the proper date for Easter, the most important day in the Christian calendar. While making his calculations the monk suggested that the years be numbered consecutively from the year of Christ's birth. This would signify the Christian era and be designated Anno Domini, or Year of the Lord. Later scholars discovered that Denis was wrong about the year of Christ's birth and that it actually took place from four to six years earlier than he believed. Strictly speaking the second millennium of the Christian era actually ended anywhere from 1994 to 1996.

Still, Denis's calculations were accepted and the system of numbering the years was gradually adopted in Christian countries over the next few hundred years.

Other nations did not accept this numbering system. The Chinese began numbering years over six thousand years ago. The Hebrew calendar is dated from the beginning of the earth—October 6, 3761 B.C.—according to tradition. Muslims use an Islamic calendar that is computed from a significant moment in the life of the prophet Muhammad, A.D. July 15, 622, when he began the hegira, his flight from Mecca to Medina.

Even among those who accept the Christian calendar there is a dispute over when the Third Millennium really begins. It is mathematically correct to state that it will not begin until the year 2001—since there was no year 0.

But none of this makes any difference at all.

The Christian calendar has become the most widely recognized in the world. It is the calendar used in all international relations and business. For Christians and non-Christians alike it is truly the international calendar.

We accept the year 2000 as the beginning of the next millennium because of what has been called "the unconscious tyranny that the decimal system exercises over our mind," our quasi-magical assumption "that round numbers have a certain significance."

A 1992 *Time* magazine article put the matter neatly: "The millennial date is an arbitrary mark on the calendar . . . The celebrated 2000, a triple tumbling of naughts, gets some of its status from humanity's fascination with zeros—

the so-called tyranny of tens that makes a neat right-angled architecture of accumulated years, time sawed off into stackable solidities like children's blocks . . . The millennium is essentially an event of the imagination."

But, arbitrary or imaginary, the millennial date is something that cannot be ignored—nor has it been.

The concept of the millennium has another and more subtle significance. A millennium is a thousand years. The only place in the Bible where a thousand-year period is mentioned prominently is in the apocalyptic Book of Revelation. In other parts of the Bible the significance of a specific or known time period is clearly downplayed with phrases like, "With the Lord one day is as a thousand years, and a thousand years as one day." Many scholars believe that the use of the word millennium should not be taken literally, but simply means a long period of time. Biblical literalists, however, insist that a millennium is a thousand years.

The Millennium with a capital M is, according to the most widely accepted interpretations, a thousand-year period of peace on earth that will be granted after Christ returns. This period of peace, however, would be granted after some truly awesome and terrifying events like Armageddon, the final battle between good and evil; the Apocalypse, a cosmic catastrophe; and the Tribulation, a seven-year period of intense persecution of Christians. While the Millennium itself is something to be welcomed, the events immediately leading up to it are to be greatly feared.

There is a general confusion between the calendar millennium of a thousand years, and the biblical Millennium. Scholars have long argued over how Europeans greeted the year 1000 at the end of the first millennium. Some believe that the Christian world was swept with an end-of-the-world panic. But evidence for such a panic is slight. At the end of the first millennium most people didn't pay much attention to calendar dates. At the end of the second millennium, however, people pay a lot of attention.

Practically everyone has a vague, general feeling that when the world's odometer ticks over to the nice round number 2000, something big is going to happen—perhaps to the world, or at least to the world as we know it.

No, we should not expect any mass frenzy with people climbing to mountaintops or falling to their knees at every clap of thunder—but it is safe to predict that apocalyptic fears will grow. All of us can expect to feel at least a twinge of uneasiness as the end of the twentieth century approaches, even if we do not believe in an imminent apocalypse. The apocalyptic speculations will be all around us, and quite impossible to avoid. And there are those who will do more than just speculate.

On March 20, 1995, a deadly nerve gas called sarin was released on the Tokyo subway system, shortly after 8 A.M. Thousands of rush-hour commuters and scores of subway workers began stumbling out of some sixteen stations in central Tokyo coughing, vomiting, and collapsing. All told, the attack left twelve people dead and more than five thousand injured. It was one of the greatest shocks the Japanese people had received since the atomic bomb was dropped on Hiroshima.

Very quickly the gas attack was traced to a relatively small and little-known religious group called Aum Shinrikyo. Aum was created around 1987 by a man who called himself Shoko Asahara. At the beginning Aum was basically a Buddhist movement and taught liberation from

In this undated picture taken before the nerve gas attack, guru Shoko Asahara, blind since birth, walks the streets of Japan with his top disciple Yoshihiro Inoue, on the right. After the attack, Inoue testified that Asahara planned the deadly attack to divert the police from a raid Asahara believed they had planned on cult headquarters.

illness and suffering and ultimate enlightenment. It also incorporated elements of the Hindu religion and stressed the practice of yoga.

Neither traditional Buddhism nor Hinduism has a strong apocalyptic vision. But Asahara began to draw inspiration from Western sources, primarily the Book of Revelation and the prophecies of Nostradamus. The group had about 10,000 devoted followers in Japan and a somewhat larger, but less well-organized number of devotees in Russia.

Asahara began to teach that the world was headed for a major catastrophe in 1999—probably mass destruction by nuclear war. He gathered his followers into fortified communities and began to stockpile weapons—including poison gas. But unlike the Davidians and most other apocalyptic groups who saw their weapons as a way to defend themselves from the outside world, Asahara directed his followers to use them to commit mass murders to make his prophecies of Armageddon come true.

After eluding police for several months Asahara was found hiding in a secret underground room in one of his fortified compounds. He claimed he was innocent and that Aum had been attacked by nerve gas sprayed by U.S. troops. By that time many of his closest associates had confessed, and a mountain of evidence linking Aum to the gas attack and other crimes had been collected.

The investigation has turned up frightening evidence that the cult was actively attempting to develop biological weapons. In 1990 three trucks sent out by the cult sprayed mists containing the deadly botulism toxin throughout the Tokyo area. U.S. naval bases in Japan were also targeted. Apparently no one was made ill, because the cult scientists did not know how to prepare and spread the toxin effectively. But they kept on trying with other deadly germ agents. Though these efforts also failed, the ease with which Asahara's agents were able to obtain the dangerous material has frightened and alerted governments throughout the world.

In many ways Aum remains a mystery. It is far from clear how what started as a rather loose association of yoga practitioners evolved into an apocalyptic movement bent on mass destruction. Certainly one factor was the way in which Asahara became locked into his own prophetic scenario, which predicted that the 1999 slide into destruction would begin in 1995. In order not to be proved wrong he had to make something dramatic happen.

In the United States there has been a growth of what has been called "secular" millennialism. This philosophy sees the Apocalypse as being man-made—brought about by social, economic, or industrial collapse, race war, nuclear war, or the actions of an oppressive and evil government. At one time groups that held these views would have seen Soviet communism as the evil force in the coming final battle—now they are more likely to blame the federal government or a shadowy "New World Order." Salvation will not come at the hands of a messiah, but in the preparations of heavily armed "patriots."

When Timothy McVeigh and Terry Nichols blew up the Alfred P. Murrah Federal Building on April 19, 1995, they appeared to believe that they were punishing the federal government for what it had done to another group of apocalyptic believers in Waco, Texas. They also hoped to help ignite an uprising among like-minded "patriots" that would bring what they considered the illegitimate federal government crashing down. McVeigh particularly had been inspired by an apocalyptic novel called *The Turner Diaries*, which has been a favorite of militia and other like-minded groups for a long time. The book describes, in detail, a mass "patriotic" revolt set off by just such a bombing.

Organizations that track the activities of the various militia and patriot groups have noted that their doctrines increasingly point to the millennium as the time when big changes will occur. The millennial uneasiness that affects all of us seems to have fueled a growth in such groups.

It is very important to repeat that there is nothing in

the Bible, either the Old or New Testament, that specifically points to the year 2000, or to any other date as the time the world will end. It is possible, by picking and choosing from various sections of the Bible and loosely interpreting selected passages, to build a case for the end of the world at about that time. But similar cases have been built for many other years. The only difference between picking the year 1843 or 1844, as the Millerites did, and the year 2000 is that 2000 is a nice round number and it sounds better.

What are the events that are supposed to lead up to the end of the world and serve as signals for the awesome event? There are, of course, many different answers given to this question. The one spelled out by Dr. John F. Walvoord, former president of the Dallas Theological Seminary, in his best-selling book *Armageddon, Oil and the Middle East Crisis*, is fairly representative.

According to Dr. Walvoord, the "Armageddon countdown" began with the establishment of the state of Israel in 1948 and with the oil politics that returned the Middle East to the center of world affairs. The return of the Jews to their ancient homeland figures importantly in the Bible.

Now there is near-chaos in the Middle East, but very soon the leader of a ten-nation confederacy of Mediterranean and European powers will impose a seven-year peace treaty protecting Israel.

At this point, Dr. Walvoord writes, "the world's death struggle" will begin. For three and a half years, a new international strongman will consolidate his power. Meanwhile the Soviet Union will attack Israel but will be defeated with divine aid. (Parts of this book were written shortly before the collapse of the Soviet Union. Somehow, it seems, the prophecies that Dr. Walvoord and so many others had interpreted completely missed this historic event.)

Continuing Dr. Walvoord's interpretation of biblical prophecy: The new world dictator will break the peace treaty, and he will be revealed as the Antichrist when he claims to be God and unleashes a terrible persecution of Christians and Jews. There will be epidemics, earthquakes, and a world war of unprecedented ferocity centered in the Israeli town of Megiddo. This is the spot that most scholars identify with the biblical "Armageddon"—the site of the predicted final battle between God and Satan. Incidentally, for the year 2000 Israel has planned to develop desolate Megiddo as a tourist site. It will probably attract a lot of visitors.

In the past the enigmatic figure of the Antichrist has been identified with German emperors, Roman Catholic popes, Napoleon, Hitler, Stalin, or any other powerful world leader whom the biblical interpreter happened to particularly dislike. Iraq's dictator Saddam Hussein was never really powerful enough to be a credible Antichrist. At the present moment interpreters of biblical prophecy do not have a strong candidate for the title.

In Dr. Walvoord's view, which is shared by many other apocalyptic writers and preachers, the world is in for a terrible time of "tribulations," starting very soon. True Christians, however, will not have to suffer through these events. They will be taken up bodily into the sky in an event called "the Rapture." There they will remain until Christ returns in all his glory, punishes the sinners, and installs a thousand-year reign of peace for Jerusalem. This Millennium will lead to a new eternal state of existence for all the faithful.

Because the ancient biblical lands of the Middle East figure so heavily in most apocalyptic belief, political events there are watched very carefully. The almost constant turmoil in that part of the world provides a steady stream of confirming evidence for those who already believe. But practically any newsworthy event—the formation of the European Economic Community, the spread of AIDS, the popularity of heavy-metal music with its use of satanic symbols—has been used as evidence that the Last Days are upon us.

In Israel itself fundamentalist Jews are also presenting their own final-days scenario, which will end with the long-awaited arrival of the Messiah. They saw the 1991 Persian Gulf War as the fulfillment of prophecies of a conflict between Babylonia, Greece, and Rome. They also see the immigration of Russian Jews to Israel as the "ingathering" of the exiles predicted in Hebrew Scriptures. In this view preparation for the Messiah will be completed with the rebuilding of the Temple in Jerusalem that was destroyed by the Romans nearly two thousand years ago. Rebuilding the Temple is the dream of some Jews and some fundamentalist Christians. But that is not government policy. The site of the Temple now contains Muslim holy places that would have to be torn down. To attempt this would undoubtedly provoke a Mideast war.

The collection of beliefs that have been lumped under the heading New Age are, in general, optimistic, cheerful, and all-inclusive. New Age devotees speak more freely of reincarnation than they do of Judgment Day. But an apocalyptic message can even be drawn out of New Age optimism if one tries hard enough. Elizabeth Clare Prophet (a name that sounds too good to be true) is a popular writer and cult leader who mixes New Age thinking with bits of Christianity and right-wing politics to come up with a message that there may well be a nuclear war before the year 2000. This is a prophecy "channeled" from the "ascended masters," including Jesus. She had her followers building bomb shelters and campaigning for the "Star Wars" missile defense system. The world may not be destroyed in the year 2000 she says, but it is best to be prepared. The breakup of the Soviet Union and the end of the nuclear confrontation of the Cold War does not seem to have altered her thinking one bit. Nor has she, or any other doomsday prophet, adequately explained how, with their great insight into the future, they managed to miss this historic change.

After writing an entire book in which I point out the errors of prophets of the past and present, it would be foolishly presumptuous to end by issuing any predictions of my own. I can only offer a bit of advice. With the approach of the end of the second millennium you are going to hear a lot of very scary things about how doomsday is just around the corner. It may be reassuring for you to recall that in one form or another all of these predictions have been made before—many, many times. Sometimes these doomsday predictions have been made by crackpots, but more often they have been made by intelligent people. Crazy or sincere, all of these predictions have one thing in common: They have all been wrong—every last one of them!

Lots of terrible things have happened in the past. There are lots of terrible things going on right now. At times even the most cheerful of us feel overwhelmed by the world's problems. It may seem as if some sort of cataclysm is inevitable, perhaps even necessary, because things have become so bad and there doesn't seem to be any earthly way of making them better. At such moments prophecies of doom can seem very reasonable and even attractive. But the experience of centuries has shown that when you wake up tomorrow, and the day after, the world with all its imperfections is still going to be there. You are still going to have to deal with it and, hopefully, make it a little better.

SELECTED BIBLIOGRAPHY

Bach, Marcus. *Strange Sects and Curious Cults.* New York: Dodd Mead, 1961.

Cayce, Edgar. *Edgar Cayce on Atlantis.* New York: Paperback Library, 1968.

Chaplin, J.P. *Rumor Fear and the Madness of Crowds.* New York: Ballantine, 1964.

Cheetham, Erick. *The Final Prophecies of Nostradamus.* New York: Putnam, 1989.

———.*The Prophecies of Nostradamus.* New York: Putnam, 1975.

Cohn, Norman. *The Pursuit of the Millennium.* Fairlawn, New Jersey: Essential Books, 1959.

De Camp, L. Sprague. *Lost Continents.* New York: Dover, 1970.

Desmond, Adrian J. *The Hot-Blooded Dinosaur.* New York: Dial, 1976.

Ebon, Martin. *Prophecy in Our Time.* New York: NAL, 1968.

Festinger, Leon; Riecken, Henry W.; and Schachter, Stanley. *When Prophecy Fails.* Minneapolis: University of Minnesota Press, 1956.

Francis, David P. *Nostradamus, Prophecies of Present Times?* New York: Sterling, 1984.

Gardner, Martin. *Fads and Fallacies in the Name of Science.* New York: Dover, 1957.

Graham, Billy. *Approaching Hoofbeats: The Four Horsemen of the Apocalypse.* New York: Avon, 1985.

Grant, Robert M. *Augustus to Constantine.* New York: Harper & Row, 1970.

Lane, Frank W. *The Elements Rage.* Philadelphia: Chilton, 1975.

Leonl, Edgar. *Nostradamus: Life and Literature.* New York: Nosbooks, 1961.

Lindsey, Hal, and Carlson, C.C. *The Late Great Planet Earth.* New York: Bantam, 1983.

———. *The Rapture: Truth or Consequences.* New York: Bantam, 1985.

Mackay, Charles. *Memoirs of Extraordinary Popular Delusions and the Madness of Crowds.* Boston: L.C. Page, 1932.

Montgomery, Ruth. *A Gift of Prophecy.* New York: Morrow, 1963.

Nichol, Francis D. *The Midnight Cry.* Takoma Park, Maryland: Review and Herald Publishing Association, 1944.

Randi, James. *The Mask of Nostradamus.* New York: Macmillan, 1990.

Robbins, Thomas and Palmer, Susan J. (eds.) *Millennium, Messiahs and Mayhem: Contemporary Apocalyptic Movements.* New York: Routledge, 1997.

Sugrue, Thomas. *There Is a River.* New York: Harper & Row, 1971.

Tompkins, Peter. *Secrets of the Great Pyramid.* New York: Doubleday, 1950.

Velikovsky, Immanuel. *Worlds in Collision.* New York: Doubleday, 1950.

Wilford, John Noble. *The Riddle of the Dinosaur.* New York: Knopf, 1985.

Winks, Robin W., ed. *The Historian as a Detective: Essays on Evidence.* New York: Harper & Row, 1969.

INDEX

Page numbers in *italics* refer to illustrations.

AIDS epidemic, 140-141
Albigenses, 19
Alexander the Great, 45, 48
Almanacs, 68, 74
Amen-Ra, 45
Anabaptists, 9-12, 19
Applewhite, Marshall Herff, 103-104
Aristotle, 119-120, 122
Arthurian legends, 55
Asahara, Shoko, *146*, 146-148
Asteroids, 84, 105-107, 109, 112, 114-118
Atlantis, 83-85

Atomic bomb, 133-134
Aum Shinrikyo, 145-148

Barringer Crater, 110-111, *111*
Black Death, 138-139, 141
Book of Daniel, 27
Book of Revelation, 13, 19, 20, 30, 132, 144, 146-147
Brahe, Tycho, 122
Branch Davidians, 23-25, 35, 147
Buddhism, 146
Burrows, William E., 115

Caesar, Julius, 49, 51, 52
Calendar, 142-143

Cassandra, 54, 56
Catherine de Médicis, 71-74
Cato, 49
Cayce, Edgar, 79-85, *81*
Centuries (Nostradamus), 66, 69-71, 73-78
Christianity, 12-18, 46, 60
Claudius Pulcher, 47, 49
Cohn, Norman, 17-18
Cold War, 98, 135
Comets, 30, 118-127, *123*, *125*
Constantine, Emperor, 46
Cournos, John, 96
Cretaceous period, 108, 113
Croesus, king of Lydia, 41-43
Cromwell, Thomas Lord, 62
Cumaean Sibyl, *57*, 57-59

Delphi, Oracle at, *39*, *40*, 41-46
Dinosaurs, 107-109, 112, 113
Dionysus Exiguus (Denis the Short), 142-143
Dixon, Jeane, 85-88, *86*
Dodona, Oracle at, 44
Donatus, 19
Donnelly, Ignatius, 126

Earthquakes, 126-129, *130*, 131
Egypt, ancient, 45, 90, 91
Epidemics, 138, 140-141
Extinction, 107-109, 112, 113

Famine, 137-138, *139*

"Fatal twenty cycle," 87, 88
Fossil record, 108
Four horsemen of the apocalypse, 132-141, *134*

Gardner, Martin, 93
Gehrels, Tom, 116
Great Pyramid of Egypt, 90-97
Greeks, ancient, 38-46, 48, 54, 55, 119-120

Hale-Bopp comet, 103, 124
Halley, Edmund, 122
Halley's comet, 122-124, *123*, *125*
Hannibal, 48
Harmony Society, 22-23
Haruspicy, *50*, 52
Heaven's Gate cult, 103-104
Hebrew prophets, 12
Henry II, king of France, 71, 73-75
Henry IV, king of France, 72
Henry VIII, king of England, 60, 62
Hermes (asteroid), 115
Hindley, Charles, 64
Hinduism, 14, 146
Hiroshima, 133, 134
Hitler, Adolf, 76, 96, 150
Huguenots, 68
Hussein, Saddam, 77, 150

Hypnotism, 80

Icarus (asteroid), 84, 114-115
Inoue, Yoshihiro, *146*
Inquisition, 67

Jehovah's Witnesses, 36-37, 94
Jesus, 12, 13, 152
Jews, 12, 60, 120, 149, 151-
152
John, Saint, 13
John of Leiden, 10-11, *11*
Josephus, 121
Julius Caesar (Shakespeare),
121-122
Justian, 15

Keech, Mrs. (pseudonym), 98,
100-102
Kelpius, Johannes, 20, 21
Kennedy, John F., 87
Khufu (Cheops), 91
Koresh, David, 23-25, *24*, 35

Labadeia, Oracle at, 44-45
Layne, Al C., 80
Livy, 48-49

Malthus, Thomas, 137-138
Marsden, Brian, 106-107, 115
Masons, 91
Mass suicide, 25, 103-104,
124
Matthys, Jan, 10
McVeigh, Timothy, 148
Menzies, Robert, 93-94

Merlin, 55-56, 63, 65
Mesmerism, 80
Meteorites, 29, 110-111, 116
Michelangelo, *57*
Millennium, 143-152
Miller, William, 26-35, *28*, 38
Millerism, 29-36, 94, 101,
118
Montanism, 17-18
Montanus, 17-19
Moravian Brethren, 19
Murray, Brian, 117

Nagasaki, 133, 134
Napoleon, 76, 150
Nettles, Bonnie Lu Trousdale,
103
New Madrid Fault, 129
New Testament, 12-14
Nichols, Terry, 148
1997 XF11 asteroid, 105-107,
115
Nixon, Richard, 87, 88
Nostradamus, 66-78, *69*, *72*,
147
Novatian, 18, 19
Nuclear weapons, 97-98, 135-
137, *136*
"Nuclear winter" theory, 112

Oklahoma City bombing, 148
Old Testament, 12, 14, 16
Omens and portents, 47-53
Oracles, 39-46

Paul, Saint, 14-15

Petrie, William Flinders, 96
Plutarch, 46
Population, 137-138
Prophet, Elizabeth Clare, 152
Pyramidology, 92-97
Pythia, 39, *40*, 41-45

Rapp, "Father" George, *22*,
    22-23
Rappites, 22-23
Romans, 12, 47-49, *50*,
    51-52, 56-59, 120-121,
    151
Rosicrucians, 21, 91
Russell, Bertrand, 97
Russell, Charles Taze, 36, 94-
    95
Rutherford, J.F., 36, 37, 95

San Andreas Fault, 129, *130*,
    131
Scrying, 70
Seventh-Day Adventists, 21,
    35, 94
Shakespeare, William, 121-
    122
Shipton, Mother, 60-65, *61*
Sibylline prophecies, 56-60,
    65
Smith, Daniel, 104
Smyth, Charles Piazzi,
    92-96

Snow, Samuel S., 33
Socrates, 45
Spurinna Vestricus, 52
Stalin, Joseph, 150
Sympathism, 51-52
Synesios, 52

Tarquinius the Proud, 58-59
Taylor, John, 92, 93
Tiresias, 55, 56
Turner Diaries, The, 148

UFOs (Unidentified Flying
    Objects), 90, 97-98, *99*,
    100-104
Unarian Society, 104
Ussher, James, 16, 78

Velikovsky, Immanuel, 126
Vespasian, 121
Vitellius, 121

Waco, Texas, 23-25, 148
Waldensians, 19
Walvoord, John F., 149-151
War, 132-137
Whiston, William, 124, 126
Wolsey, Cardinal, 61-62
Woman in the Wilderness,
    The, 21, 22

Zimmerman, Johann Jacob, 20